BE ACCOUNTABLE!

RACHEL NicANTHONY

Contents

INTRODUCTION

Leadership entails more than just occupying a position of power; it also entails accepting the responsibility that comes with it. The demand for accountable leadership has never been greater in a world where enterprises must navigate an ever-changing terrain. This introduction establishes the groundwork for a thorough examination of responsible leadership, diving into its definition, historical relevance, and critical role in establishing successful and sustainable companies.

Defining Accountable Leadership

Accountable leadership is more than a catchphrase; it is a revolutionary strategy to directing individuals and organizations to achievement. Accountable leadership, at its foundation, entails accepting responsibility for one's actions, decisions, and the ultimate consequences of a team or organization. It goes beyond traditional concepts of power and places an emphasis on transparency, ethical behavior, and a commitment to ongoing growth. Accountable leaders recognize that their effect extends beyond the bottom line. It pervades company culture, affecting team behavior and generating an environment of trust and innovation. As we begin this investigation into accountable leadership, it is critical to recognize its varied character and the enormous influence it can have on individuals, teams, and whole organizations.

Accountable Leadership's Historical Context

To properly understand the core of responsible leadership, consider past personalities who embraced its ideas. Leaders like Mahatma Gandhi, Nelson Mandela, and Abraham Lincoln have made an everlasting impression on history not just for their successes but also for their unflinching dedication to responsibility. Nelson Mandela, for example, returned from decades of jail with an unblemished soul. His dedication to reconciliation and nation-building demonstrated a deep sense of responsibility, establishing a pattern for accountable leadership. Similarly, Lincoln's ability to lead a nation through the difficult time of the Civil War with honesty and responsibility continues to serve as a model for leaders facing hardship.

These historical examples demonstrate how accountable leadership is ageless. It is not a passing fad, but rather a pillar of long-term success, demonstrating that the ideas inherent in responsible leadership are not limited by time or circumstance.

The Accountability Imperative in Modern Leadership

The need for accountable leadership has never been more apparent in today's corporate scene, which is marked by fast technical breakthroughs, globalization, and enormous difficulties. Organizations operate in a world where leaders' activities are analyzed not just by internal stakeholders, but also by a worldwide audience linked via social media and instantaneous communication channels. Accountable leadership protects organizations against ethical failures and business crises that can irreversibly harm their brand. It goes beyond crisis management to create a foundation for long-term growth and innovation. Accountable leadership develops as a strategic need rather than a discretionary leadership style in an era where customers want openness, workers seek purpose, and investors analyze company governance. This book intends to investigate the various facets of accountable leadership, offering ideas, tactics, and real-world examples to help leaders negotiate the difficulties of today's corporate context.

The book's ensuing chapters are precisely prepared to take readers on a thorough journey of accountable leadership. Each chapter focuses on a different aspect, providing practical insights, case studies, and effective recommendations. The fundamentals of accountable leadership, including leadership styles and basic values, will be deconstructed to give readers with a robust framework. Values and ethics, which are essential components of accountable leadership, will be thoroughly examined, with an emphasis on their impact in decision-making and organizational culture. Developing an accountability culture, creating and attaining goals, and embracing openness will be shown as critical building blocks for effective leadership. The book will dive into the complexities of accountability, trust, and continuous improvement, viewing them as continuing processes rather than isolated events. As leaders navigate unknown territory in an unpredictable environment, special emphasis will be placed on responsibility in crisis management.

Chapters on overcoming accountability problems and case studies on real-life instances will give readers with practical skills and encouragement. The investigation will conclude with a chapter that looks ahead, identifying new trends and addressing the future of accountable leadership. As we begin on this journey, I hope that the lessons presented in these pages will not only enlighten but also inspire leaders at all levels. Accountable leadership has the ability to raise your influence and produce persistent success, whether you are a seasoned executive, an aspiring manager, or an entrepreneur defining the course of your enterprise. According to John C. Maxwell, "a leader is someone who knows the way, goes the way, and shows the way." This book's goal is to provide leaders with the information, resources, and motivation they need to embody accountable leadership, paving the road for a more resilient, ethical, and prosperous future.

Why is leadership accountability important?

Accountability is vital in leadership because it ensures that your team is working toward a unified objective and following through on their promises. It fosters trust and mutual respect between the leader and their team. Employees will have more faith in your leadership if leaders are held accountable for their actions and understand the implications of failing to fulfill expectations. This form of responsibility also encourages creativity among your team members, which may lead to greater success in the long term.

What is the difference between leadership responsibility and accountability?

Becoming a great leader begins with a knowledge of the characteristics that distinguish great leaders and the common talents that many share. In a remote working environment, the expectations on leaders have risen, but the requirement for performance has not. Accountability may take various forms, including as objectives, deadlines, and milestones, but at its foundation, it is simply holding individuals accountable for results. This may appear easy and obvious, but in my experience as an entrepreneur and leader, it is frequently the most significant impediment to success.

Why should a good leader be held accountable?

Accountability is an important aspect of leadership. It is, in essence, the act of holding yourself accountable to others. You must be able to hold yourself responsible for your actions and choices, as well as the actions and decisions of those who report to you, in order to be an effective leader. People who do not feel accountable will not accept personal responsibility for themselves and will not be held accountable by others or management for their own or others on their team's activities. It is based on assumptions. It all comes down to being open with everyone involved about what you want from them and why. People who feel accountable for their acts take responsibility of them and can readily correct any mistakes they make.

According to a recent research conducted by Professor Gary Latham of the Australian Graduate School of Management, corporate executives who exhibited the traits of accountability and integrity outperformed their colleagues. So, what attributes and behaviors distinguish accountable leaders? These are five characteristics that I feel are prevalent in accountable leadership.

5 Ways to Show Leadership Accountability and Instill It in Others

Many behaviors are modeled by responsible leaders and their teams in the interest of developing a higher performance culture.

1. Communication is a key characteristic of an accountable leader.

It is critical to be able to communicate effectively in order to achieve team alignment and clarity of purpose. People must believe that their leaders are capable of providing clear guidance. When communication is ambiguous, teams lose focus and become disengaged.

Are your team's expectations clear?

If you ask someone to do something and they don't do it, it's possible that they didn't hear or comprehend what you said, or that their attention was elsewhere. This can lead to confusion and dissatisfaction, both of which will undercut the effectiveness of your efforts. Creating feedback opportunities in your team is a wonderful method to discover where communication is failing and how to fix it. Leaders of distant teams must consider the most effective communication method. Any technological solutions must promote accountability and assist monitor priority areas and tasks to ensure alignment. Building trust in this setting necessitates consciously concentrating on providing opportunities for your staff to share an experience, get to know one another, and develop a feeling of camaraderie and collaboration.

2. Delegation is a trait of an accountable leader.

Hovering over an employee's shoulder (even remotely) is not an effective strategy to develop a good team culture based on accountability. Concentrate on being organized and assisting your team in understanding their priority areas and how you can help them achieve their goals. People who feel accountable for their acts take responsibility of them and can readily correct any mistakes they make. This fosters trust between leaders and their teams. If you want to be an effective leader, make your team members feel responsibility for their activities. Focus on holding the team to the same standards that you would, and keep them involved in whatever objective you've established as a team.

3. Listening is a quality of an accountable leader.

Listening pathways, whether remote-first or office-first, are now a key component of strong safety leadership. Creating an atmosphere in which your team is heard, concerns are acknowledged, and opportunities for growth are pursued is a critical component of building an accountability culture. According to a recent McKinsey research, teams prefer leaders who empower others and foster an open environment over those who exercise authoritarian or consultative leadership. The requirement to demonstrate that you are a helpful and caring leader has grown significantly. This is followed by being employee-focused, which must begin with listening. Creating this feedback platform allows teams to better understand one another, the variables influencing their performance, and how we may improve. A critical component of accountability is building trust in the group so that the team may be honest and vulnerable. Better outcomes will result from a shared feeling of ownership of team goals and a robust feedback environment.

How frequently do you check in with your team right now?

- What technologies do you use to offer useful data to distant managers?

- Is everyone aware of any potential issues that might jeopardize our objectives? Is anyone suffering or on the verge of burnout?

4. Ownership is a trait of an accountable leader.

In terms of leadership responsibility, we must first be accountable for our own actions. Self-accountability requires leaders to establish high criteria for themselves and plan out how they will achieve them on paper. If you want your team to be held accountable for their activities, we must first hold ourselves accountable. Accept responsibility for your errors. If you make a mistake, accept responsibility and make repairs as quickly as feasible. When you accept responsibility for something that goes wrong, your team will regard it as proof that you can be honest and learn from your errors. You haven't given up striving to get better.

5. Characteristics of an Accountable Leader

Invest in Your People. You must be willing to invest in individuals in order for them to feel valued and respected. Employees will feel more committed in their job and more accountable for how they do if you show them trust by providing them responsibilities and chances. Employees will want to take greater ownership of their responsibilities and so become more accountable for their activities as they feel more valued by their employers.

How are you getting to know your team as a remote leader?

- What is their goal, and what motivates them to succeed in their position?
- Do you need to include some face-to-face encounters in your quarterly plans?

The significance of responsibility for a leader

Accountability has various advantages. It is not just a tool for helping you reach your own objectives, but it also motivates those around you. Results must be tracked, measured, and reviewed on a regular basis. You must constantly evaluate your performance and think of methods to enhance it.

Improved collaboration

Accountability empowers employees to take responsibility of their work and allows them to collaborate toward a common objective. This boosts worker productivity and dedication, allowing them to work more effectively and productively toward reaching organizational goals.

Alignment

Accountability works so effectively because it brings everyone on the same page and makes it easy for everyone to understand what has to be done and how they fit into the greater goal. Many of the most productive teams I've worked with have an unwritten understanding to first seek input and approval from others.

Engagement

Setting clear standards and giving teams a true purpose is an effective method to boost employee engagement. Setting these criteria and then holding them each month fosters a Culture of Accountability from leaders, assuring the creation of a strong performance culture.

Productivity

When you consider the cost of not doing anything, it's easy to appreciate the value of responsibility. Failure to follow through on pledges can have major implications, such as missed deadlines and losing out on key activities. If deadlines are missed, standards are not stated, and there is no responsibility, your staff will get disengaged.

Effective leadership is driven by a culture of accountability.

It is simple to establish the foundation for an accountability culture, but it is more difficult to sustain one. And not every industry has perfected the art. According to the graph below, the travel, transportation, and logistics businesses fail to incorporate accountability into their culture. You must maintain a culture of responsibility after it has been established. Without an established culture, your workers will likely begin to see their time as their own and will be less concerned with developing a culture that fosters accountability. So, what can leaders do to sustain an accountability-inspiring culture? The first thing a leader should do is make sure his or her team knows the significance of accountability.

It is critical that you, as a leader, ensure that everyone understands their own obligations. Then point folks in the direction of what they can do to become more accountable for themselves. You may assist your staff understand their duties and how they fit into the bigger picture as you work with them.

Finally, here are some things you can do right immediately as a leader to assist you keep on track and accountable:

- Check-ins should be scheduled.
- Feedback sessions should be held on a regular basis.
- Clear strategic goals that are aligned with monthly emphasis areas (OKRs or a variation on this might work well)
- Be explicit about your goals' priority; not all goals may be equal.
- Utilize technology to improve alignment and transparency so that everyone is aware of priority areas.
- Micromanage, but set clear objectives and priorities.
- Establish deadlines.

Historical Examples of Accountable Leadership

Accountable leadership examples from history give unique insights into the influence of responsibility on individuals, organizations, and even nations. We may take lessons from the acts and decisions of former leaders by studying their actions and judgments. Here, we look at several historical personalities and situations that demonstrate accountable leadership.

1. Abraham Lincoln: Accepting Accountability in Times of Crisis

Abraham Lincoln, the 16th President of the United States, is often regarded as a model of responsible leadership, notably during the American Civil War. Lincoln made tough judgments with a strong sense of duty in the face of enormous pressure and disagreement. His dedication to preserve the Union while negotiating the complications of emancipation demonstrated a leader who was prepared to accept responsibility for the repercussions of his actions. Lincoln's responsibility was clear in his speeches, such as the Gettysburg Address, in which he emphasized that the government was "of the people, by the people, and for the people." This reinforced his idea that leaders owed allegiance to the people they served. Lincoln's approach to responsibility lay the groundwork for the nation's rebuilding.

2. Nelson Mandela: Forgiveness and Responsibility

Nelson Mandela, South Africa's former President and anti-apartheid revolutionary, showed responsible leadership via his dedication to peace and forgiveness. Mandela came from jail after 27 years with a vision of a unified South Africa free of racial oppression. Mandela's focus on reconciliation demonstrated his grasp of accountability not only to his followers but also to the larger goal of national unity. He formed the Truth and Reconciliation Commission to provide a forum for victims and perpetrators of apartheid-era crimes to openly address the past. Mandela's accountable leadership established the framework for a peaceful transition to democracy, avoiding a spiteful route that may have resulted in much more chaos.

3. Winston Churchill: Wartime Decision-Making Accountability

Winston Churchill, the British Prime Minister during WWII, exemplified responsible leadership by making bold decisions and being firm in his views. Faced with the immediate prospect of Nazi attack, Churchill had to make difficult decisions, frequently carrying the weight of responsibility for the fate of the British people. One of the most noteworthy examples is Churchill's unwillingness to negotiate with Adolf Hitler in the early stages of the war, despite the severe circumstances. His commitment to the ideas of liberty and democracy triumphed over short-term practicality. Churchill's leadership not only galvanized the British people, but also made a crucial contribution to the Allied triumph.

4. Martin Luther King Jr.: Moral Accountability in Leadership

Martin Luther King Jr., the legendary leader of the American civil rights movement, exemplified moral responsibility in the quest of justice and equality. His support for nonviolent resistance and civil disobedience stemmed from his conviction that leaders must be held accountable not just for their acts but also for the ethical ideals they promote. King's renowned "I Have a Dream" speech not only expressed his goal for racial equality, but it also held a mirror to the nation's conscience, urging leaders to hold systematic racism responsible. His dedication to nonviolent protest and moral accountability became a guiding force for social movements all across the world.

5. Deng Xiaoping: Chinese Economic Accountability

Deng Xiaoping, China's supreme leader from the late 1970s to the early 1990s, instituted economic reforms that turned the country into a global economic powerhouse. Deng's pragmatic approach to Chinese-style socialism emphasized accountability for economic outcomes and brought millions out of poverty. Deng's responsible leadership was demonstrated by his willingness to experiment with market-oriented changes despite probable internal Communist Party opposition. His emphasis on outcomes and responsibility opened the path for China's economic comeback, proving how leaders can be held accountable for the well-being of their populace even within the restrictions of a single-party system.

6. Mahatma Gandhi: The Importance of Personal Accountability

Through his ideology of peaceful resistance and civil disobedience, Mahatma Gandhi, the leader of the Indian freedom struggle, embodied personal accountability. Gandhi's dedication to truth (Satya) and nonviolence (Ahimsa) exemplified a leader who held himself to the highest moral standards. As he lived the values he promoted, Gandhi's accountability was extremely personal. His capacity to accept personal responsibility for his acts, whether by protest fasting or leading by example, encouraged a country to seek accountability in its quest for independence. Gandhi's example highlighted how personal accountability may drive transformational social change.

Examples of responsible leadership throughout history provide a rich tapestry of lessons for today's leaders. Whether confronted with war, social injustice, economic transformation, or personal accountability, these leaders negotiated complexity with a sense of duty that extended beyond individual interests. We discover fundamental concepts that may guide leaders in today's dynamic and complex situations as we examine their behaviors and decisions. Aspiring leaders may gain a better knowledge of responsibility and its transformational potential on individuals, organizations, and society at large by drawing inspiration from these historical personalities.

THE FOUNDATIONS OF ACCOUNTABLE LEADERSHIP

The notion of responsibility is a cornerstone in the ever-changing environment of leadership, shaping the character and performance of leaders across numerous areas. Accountable leadership extends beyond the surface obligations of a position to the basic concepts that drive leaders in cultivating a culture of trust, transparency, and continual progress. We deconstruct the important aspects that contribute to the formation of leaders that not only guide their teams to success but also serve as examples of honesty and responsibility in this investigation of the foundations of responsible leadership.

Recognizing Leadership Styles

A comprehensive awareness of distinct leadership styles and their influence on organizational dynamics is at the heart of accountable leadership. Accountability is not a one-size-fits-all idea, and leaders must acknowledge this. Different situations may necessitate different leadership styles, ranging from authoritarian to collaborative. The goal is to tailor one's leadership style to the team's requirements and the issues at hand. Transformational leadership, servant leadership, and genuine leadership theories all give frameworks for developing accountability. Transformational leaders encourage and empower their colleagues to attain their maximum potential, whereas servant leaders put others' needs first. Authentic leaders, on the other hand, lead with sincerity and integrity, ensuring that their actions are consistent with their principles. Accountable leaders may build a pleasant and successful work environment by recognizing these various leadership styles.

Accountability is one of the most important characteristics that a person may have and demonstrate in work. It will assist you in being a better leader, employee, and individual. It makes no difference why you want to imbibe this feature; the method is the same for everyone. As a result, wherever you go, this attribute will make you responsible and accountable for your activities. Do you want to start your accountability journey? Do you believe you are well prepared and informed? If you answered yes, do you know what the fundamental principles of accountability are? Probably not, but don't worry, since that is exactly what we will cover in this chapter.

What impact does accountability have on others around you?

Accountability is a leadership quality that necessitates accepting responsibility for your actions, decisions, and mistakes. And once the leader accepts responsibility, the team will follow. But how would this benefit your staff or others around you? So, for a better understanding, consider the following suggestions:

- It fosters team togetherness since everyone understands that they are jointly responsible for what happens.
- Accountability will promote communication among team members.
- Accountability increases your company's workflow by making people feel more accountable for their activities.
- It allows people or workers to reflect on their behavior and improve.
- It also instills honesty in your team and allows you to adequately recognize positive efforts.
- Accountability's Fundamental Principles

Now that you understand what accountability is and why it is important in the workplace, it is time to go over the fundamental concepts. Consider these essential values to be the skeleton of a responsible personality. You will comprehend what accountability implies if you have a firm grasp on these ideas.

Take a look at this list of all the concepts of accountability, along with a concise explanation:

In the ever-changing world of organizational management, accountable leadership shines brightly. Personal responsibility, transparency, and ethical decision-making are all intertwined in this dynamic idea. In this investigation, we dig into the basic concepts that serve as the foundation of responsible leadership, providing a complete plan for leaders seeking to foster an accountability culture inside their teams and organizations.

1. Personal Accountability is Based on Personal Responsibility

Accountable leadership starts with a strong commitment to

personal accountability. Leaders must accept responsibility for their actions, decisions, and the influence they have on the team and company. This principle entails a thorough knowledge that one's job extends beyond power; it includes a responsibility to act ethically, make educated judgments, and be accountable for the results. When leaders accept personal responsibility, they create a culture in which others feel empowered to do the same.

2. Transparent Communication: Promoting Trust and Openness

Transparency is a critical component of accountable leadership. Leaders should communicate with their teams freely and honestly, offering insight into decision-making processes and company goals. Transparency promotes trust and encourages a collaborative atmosphere. Leaders who communicate information, whether favorable or bad, foster an environment in which team members feel valued and informed, which leads to increased engagement and commitment.

3. Ethical Decision-Making: Charting a Course with Integrity

Accountable leaders' moral compass is formed by ethics. Ethical decision-making entails making decisions that are consistent with the ideals of honesty, integrity, and fairness. Leaders must manage complicated situations, frequently confronted with ethical quandaries that demand careful deliberation. Prioritizing ethical decision-making builds trust among team members and guarantees that the organization runs with integrity, winning respect from internal and external stakeholders.

4. Clarity in Expectations and Standards: Creating a Success Framework

Accountable leaders establish clear goals and objectives for themselves and their teams. This concept calls for the establishment of roles, responsibilities, and performance measures. When expectations are clear, team members understand what is expected of them, which reduces uncertainty and fosters responsibility. Clear standards also serve as a foundation for evaluating performance, allowing leaders to celebrate accomplishments while addressing areas in need of development.

5. Fostering Growth and Development Through Feedback and Recognition

Leadership responsibility includes giving constructive comments and recognizing others. A crucial idea is to foster an environment in which feedback is considered as a tool for progress rather than as a source of criticism. Leaders should provide timely and precise feedback, recognizing achievements while emphasizing areas for growth. Recognition is a strong motivator, rewarding great conduct and fostering a culture of continual growth within the team.

6. Empowering Others: Creating an Accountability Culture

Accountable leaders empower their teams by instilling a feeling of responsibility and autonomy in them. Delegating duties and giving team members decision-making authority not only promotes individual progress but also improves the organization's accountability fabric. Leaders who empower others foster a collaborative environment in which each team member has a personal interest in the collective effort's success.

7. Adaptability and Resilience: Thriving in a Changing Environment

Accountable leaders are resilient and flexible in the face of change. The corporate landscape is ever-changing, and great executives maintain their cool in the face of adversity. This principle entails accepting change, learning from setbacks, and displaying resilience in the pursuit of corporate goals. Leaders that demonstrate flexibility inspire trust in their colleagues, fostering a culture in which setbacks are perceived as opportunities for progress.

8. Values Consistency: Aligning Actions with Principles

Value consistency is a fundamental element of accountable leadership. Leaders must ensure that their behaviors are consistent with the principles they promote, maintaining integrity in every decision and contact. This principle entails adhering to ethical norms, remaining transparent, and maintaining a commitment to responsibility even in the face of hardship. Value consistency fosters trust and credibility, positioning the leader as a trustworthy and principled guide.

9. Inclusivity and Diversity: Capitalizing on Differences

Accountable leaders understand the importance of inclusiveness and diversity on their teams. This approach entails creating an environment in which varied viewpoints are not just welcomed, but actively sought. Inclusive leadership fosters creativity, innovation, and a more comprehensive knowledge of complicated challenges. Leaders that promote diversity display a dedication to justice and equality, fostering an environment in which every employee feels valued and responsibility for the organization's success.

10. Evolving with the Leadership Landscape Through Continuous Learning

Continuous learning is an essential component of accountable leadership. Leaders must commit to personal and professional growth, remaining current on industry trends, best practices in leadership, and new difficulties. This continuous search of information enables leaders to modify their strategy, make educated judgments, and motivate their staff to look forward. Continuous learning ensures that accountable leaders maintain their effectiveness in an ever-changing reality.

Accountable leadership orchestrates the harmonic collaboration of individuals toward a common vision in the symphony of corporate achievement. The aforementioned basic principles provide a complete framework for executives wanting to foster accountability within their teams and organizations. Leaders may create a culture where accountability is not a demand but a shared commitment by embracing personal responsibility, transparency, ethical decision-making, and other critical concepts, moving the firm toward long-term growth and success.

Leadership accountability skills

Leadership accountability is an essential component of good leadership, since it drives achievement and fosters a culture of responsibility within a company. Strong accountability abilities in leaders contribute considerably to the general health and success of their teams and the company as a whole. We will dig into the important leadership accountability abilities and their influence on establishing a successful and sustainable work environment in this exploration.

The 5 Cs of Leadership Accountability

Accountability is a key component of effective leadership, and great leaders recognize the value of accepting responsibility for their actions and decisions. To gain a thorough understanding of leadership responsibility, examine the notion via the 5 Cs: Clarity, Communication, Consistency, Consequences, and Continuous Improvement.

1. Clarity

Leadership responsibility begins with a well-defined vision and expectations. Leaders must communicate their aims, beliefs, and ambitions in a way that their team can understand. This clarity lays the groundwork for a shared understanding of the organization's goal, increasing team members' sense of togetherness. Leaders must clearly define expectations for individual and group performance, leaving no opportunity for misunderstanding. Accountability becomes more possible when everyone is on the same page about what needs to be done and how success will be judged. Setting specific, quantifiable, and attainable objectives is an important part of leadership responsibility. Leaders should collaborate with their teams to develop objectives that are consistent with the broader vision. Communicate the goals clearly and make sure that each team member knows their role in accomplishing them.

2. Communication

Effective leadership accountability is hard to achieve in the absence of open and honest communication. Leaders must foster an environment in which team members feel free to communicate their opinions, concerns, and ideas. Regular communication channels, such as team meetings, one-on-one conversations, and feedback sessions, are essential for establishing an accountability culture. Leaders should not only convey their expectations, but also actively listen to their team members' viewpoints. This two-way communication builds trust and ensures that everyone understands their roles and the organization's general vision.

Constructive feedback is an effective strategy for increasing accountability. Leaders should offer timely and detailed feedback to their team members in order to encourage them toward progress. This feedback loop emphasizes the significance of responsibility by allowing individuals to see the immediate consequence of their actions and receive advice on how to improve their performance.

3. Consistency

Accountable leadership demonstrates consistency. Leaders must consistently apply their values and standards in a variety of scenarios. Inconsistency causes confusion and undermines confidence. Leaders demonstrate their commitment to accountability by displaying a consistent approach to decision-making and problem-solving. Leaders are not immune from accountability. They must demonstrate the behavior that they demand of their team members. When leaders constantly accept responsibility for their actions, confess mistakes, and commit to continuous improvement, they establish a powerful example that fosters similar conduct in their teams.

4. Consequences

Accountability entails keeping individuals accountable for their behavior, which may need repercussions. However, leaders must ensure that the repercussions are fair, reasonable, and consistent with company principles. Arbitrary or punitive actions can erode confidence and impede accountability. Leaders should create clear performance objectives and disclose the potential repercussions of failing to meet them. They accomplish this by establishing a framework that promotes accountability without resorting to severe or inconsistent disciplinary procedures. Along with repercussions for poor performance, leaders should acknowledge and reward accountability. Acknowledging and applauding accomplishments, especially when they are the consequence of a commitment to responsibility, reinforces the good habits that leaders strive to instill in their teams.

5. Constant Improvement

Accountable leaders understand that errors are chances for development. When mistakes occur, the emphasis should not be only on assigning blame, but on determining what went wrong and how to improve. Leaders that support a culture of continuous improvement help their teams to be resilient and adaptable.

Adaptability is critical for long-term success in today's volatile business climate. Leaders must be held accountable not just for their activities under stable conditions, but also for efficiently managing change. This necessitates a willingness to rethink methods, learn from mistakes, and modify course as needed.

Accountability in leadership is a complicated notion that includes clarity, communication, consistency, sanctions, and ongoing progress. By adopting the 5 Cs, leaders can develop a culture that not only holds people accountable for their actions, but also fosters a feeling of shared responsibility for the organization's overall performance. Accountable leaders can motivate their teams to excellence while retaining trust, transparency, and a commitment to continuous improvement by incorporating these concepts

THE ROLE OF VALUES AND ETHICS

The importance of values and ethics in leadership is critical to developing a long-term and influential company culture. Values and ethics serve as the foundation for accountable leadership, affecting decision-making processes, directing conduct, and forming an organization's moral compass. We will dig into the complex link between values, ethics, and effective leadership in this in-depth examination.

Defining Leadership Values and Ethics

Values are the fundamental ideas and concepts that influence the activities and decisions of an individual or an organization. They serve as the culture's basis and define what is considered significant. Values are the compass that governs conduct and sets the tone for the entire team in leadership. Ethics, on the other hand, refers to the moral standards that guide an individual's or a group's behavior. It entails discriminating between good and wrong and making judgments that are consistent with recognized behavioral norms.

Leadership Values Integration

Effective leaders understand the significance of incorporating values into their leadership style. They not only mold their own acts, but also the conduct and attitudes of those they lead. Here are some examples of how values influence leadership:

1. Defining corporate Culture:
The principles that leaders embrace create the foundation of corporate culture. Leaders who embody and promote certain values foster a common sense of purpose and identity throughout the business.

2. offering a Framework for assessing Options:
Values serve as decision-making criteria, offering a framework for assessing options. Leaders that prioritize ethical standards make judgments that are consistent with the ideals of the organization, establishing trust and credibility.

3. Inspiring and Motivating Teams:

Values help to create a feeling of purpose and motivation among team members. Individuals are more likely to be motivated and interested in their job when they understand and resonate with the principles of their leaders.

4. Establishing Trust:

Trust is the foundation of good leadership. When values are regularly respected, they foster trust among teams and with external stakeholders. Trust is a delicate factor that, once damaged, may be difficult to repair; hence, maintaining a values-driven approach is critical.

Leadership Ethical Decision-Making

Accountable leadership requires ethical decision-making. Leaders confront a plethora of decisions, and their choices affect not just the business but also the individuals inside it. Ethical decision-making entails the following steps:

1. examine Stakeholder Impact:

Leaders must examine the impact of their actions on numerous stakeholders, including as workers, customers, and the larger community. Ethical leaders put the greater good ahead of short-term benefits.

2. Balancing Conflicting Interests:

During decision-making, leaders may come across conflicting interests. Ethical executives manage these issues by pursuing equitable solutions that are consistent with the ideals of the company.

3. Integrity:

Integrity is essential for ethical leadership. Leaders that maintain high moral standards in their acts and decisions win their colleagues' respect and appreciation, promoting a healthy and ethical workplace culture.

Ethical Accountability Case Studies

Examining real-world instances of ethical leadership decision-making gives useful insights into the practical application of values and ethics. One such example is the 1982 Tylenol problem at Johnson & Johnson. In the face of product tampering that resulted in multiple deaths, Johnson & Johnson CEO James Burke made the brave choice to recall 31 million bottles of Tylenol, costing the business millions of dollars. This prompt and ethical approach placed customer safety over profit, demonstrating the company's dedication to its ideals and, as a result, enhancing its reputation over time.

Microsoft's dedication to diversity and inclusion is another shining example. Microsoft has aggressively developed an inclusive culture, acknowledging the importance of many viewpoints, under the leadership of Satya Nadella. Nadella has changed Microsoft into a more inclusive and inventive workplace by emphasizing principles such as respect and empathy.

Keeping Transparency and Confidentiality in Check

While openness is essential for accountable leadership, leaders frequently confront the difficulty of reconciling transparency with the requirement for secrecy. Maintaining trust and ethical standards requires striking the appropriate balance. Here's how leaders may strike a careful balance:

1. Transparent Communication:

Transparent communication is freely exchanging information, especially when it affects the team or the company. Leaders must convey their judgments, reasoning, and possible implications.

2. Maintaining Confidentiality:

Confidentiality is essential in some situations, such as sensitive corporate plans or personnel affairs. Leaders must explain the necessity of secrecy to their teams while still being open about the larger aims and principles that guide their decisions.

3. Establishing a Culture of Trust:

Trust serves as a link between openness and secrecy. Leaders who constantly display integrity and uphold ethical standards foster a culture in which team members recognize the importance of secrecy and respect openness in other elements of leadership.

The importance of values and ethics in leadership is critical to organizational success and sustainability. Leaders that focus and exemplify ethical ideals foster a healthy company culture, motivate their staff, and negotiate difficult situations with honesty. The marriage of values and ethics is the foundation of accountable leadership, promoting trust, motivation, and long-term success. As leaders wrestle with the intricacies of decision-making, a firm commitment to values guarantees that their choices have a positive and long-term impact on both the business and its stakeholders.

What is Ethical Leadership? Attributes, Traits, & Examples

Many of us will have witnessed ethical leadership, while others will have witnessed a lack of ethical leadership in our professional life. The type of leadership style in place will be determined by who is at the very top. Employees are empowered by ethical leaders who inspire, develop, and foster a culture of trust and respect. It's becoming clear that the future of business, and the future of driving change in our workplace practices, will be more ethical leadership that aims to produce outcomes in a more holistic approach. But what exactly is ethical leadership, and why is it so vital in today's economic environment? From providing winning teams to lower turnover, improved productivity, and employee loyalty, ethical leadership offers several benefits that we will discuss in depth in the following guide. We will delve deeper into the realm of ethical leadership, what it is, why it is so essential, ethical leadership principles, and look at some instances of ethical leaders in industry today.

What exactly is ethical leadership?

Ethical leadership occurs when company executives act appropriately both within and outside of the office, in accordance with recognized principles and values. Ethical leadership is about exhibiting strong moral beliefs that will call out wrongdoings (even if it may not help their business) and showcasing what's right via their words and deeds. Ethical leaders set an example for the rest of the organization and want their actions and words to be respected and followed with the same convictions by their employees. You might argue that many of today's politicians and CEOs are terrible examples of ethical leadership, but there are also good instances of leaders in both industries where ethical leadership has been a crucial factor in their success.

The value of ethical leadership

Ethical leadership provides several advantages, which have been investigated by clinical experts and emphasized in numerous successful company tales. Here are a few instances of the advantages of ethical leadership.

Brand image enhancement

Maintaining moral brand standards is even more critical now in a digital, fast-paced environment when a single picture may damage a business. Ethical leadership may drastically boost brand image in the eyes of bystanders by behaving and acting appropriately.

Staff morale has improved.

Ethical leadership entails encouraging, motivating, and holding employees accountable for their job. When this occurs, greater corporate success is possible since people are more satisfied at work.

Positive work environment

If ethical leaders may have an impact on results, they can also have an impact on workplace culture. Where ethical leaders may improve the workplace to inspire and motivate others to follow excellent ethical behavior is by walking the walk and talking the talk.

Customer devotion

Customers demand more than just a "good product"; they want their purchases to be ethical as well. A company that can demonstrate ethical choices and judgments will profit. In the United Kingdom, for example, Millican aspires to "re-use as much recycled material as possible (88%) in the construction of their items and inspire climate awareness initiatives through our working practices."

Employee loyalty

Ethical leadership is about establishing trust with your people and then regaining that trust. Increased employee loyalty is more than possible if workers feel less intimidated and less opposed to the company's direction.

Increased recruiting

With more individuals working remotely, finding the proper

people with both ethical and moral ideals is critical in order to mirror those of the business and the leadership and provide equal service to the firm.

Obtaining investment

Potential investment is boosted when a company stands for clear ethical and moral values since it instills trust in investors in general. They are making a positive overall impression and brand image in the market. The broad image of ethical leadership is that it promotes a corporation that supports good causes and looks after its employees. This promotes a good image of the company, its employees, and the product or service it produces.

Principles of ethical leadership

We've talked a lot about ethical leadership, but it requires a framework to be followed for it to be meaningful. FATHER is the most often identified paradigm for explaining the ideas of ethical leadership. This will now be broken down.

Fairness

Fairness is a fundamental ethical leadership characteristic. Fairness is concerned with how individuals interact with one another and expect to be treated. We expect to be treated fairly, and we treat people fairly in return. Favoritism has no place in fairness because the circumstance is the same for everyone, and fairness is also tied to how you discipline someone. If two persons commit the same mistake, they must be penalized equally.

Accountability

Being held responsible for poor actions and blunders is a positive trait; it is also a key characteristic of ethical leadership. Some of us make mistakes and move on swiftly, while others blame someone or even the gods. Taking responsibility for a mistake, on the other hand, demonstrates that you are a strong, well-rounded leader that others want to follow.

Trust

A great team cannot exist without trust running through it. How can you be expected to finish something if you don't believe your colleagues won't utilize it, claim it as their own, and so on? Trust is fundamental to how we live and work; we want others around us to trust us and help us build high-performing teams, whether in the military, football teams, or teams inside your organization.

Honesty

We all like it when individuals are truthful with us, but what does it mean when our leaders are? It fosters an atmosphere in which we may openly debate significant concerns. This immediately affects trust, and if you can't be honest with someone, trust is damaged, and you won't be able to hear the truth in that talk either.

Equality

There has been considerable debate about equality in our daily lives, yet equality is the foundation of our survival and enjoyment. Nobody likes to be treated unequally, and prejudice against a wide range of things serves nothing to aid our survival or pleasure. Discrimination demonstrates that you are working with someone who is not well-rounded, ethical, or moral. Working with ethical leaders means that the playing field is equal in their views, which develops a mentality that approaches these challenges with the same amount of respect as the rest of the team.

Respect

The skill of courteous disagreement is no longer practiced. There are hundreds of YouTube videos aimed to teach us how we can do it, demonstrating how poisonous some global discourses have become. Respect is defined as showing consideration for the other person's wishes, feelings, and rights, even if you disagree with them. A true comprehension of humanity entails demonstrating the capacity to examine the ideas and thoughts of others, as well as why there are disparities in opinions and points of view.

Characteristics of ethical leaders

We have obtained a concept of ethical leadership - "when business leaders demonstrate appropriate conduct" - and have come to appreciate what the principles of ethical leadership look like using the FATHER acronym. So, how do ethical leaders put these ideals into action? Here are a few highlights.

Provides an excellent example

One of the most crucial parts of ethical leadership is to walk the walk as well as talk the talk. Ethical leaders would hold their staff to the same high standards that they hold themselves to on a regular basis. Would they do the work they're asking someone else to do? The response should be yes.

Everyone is treated with same respect.

Respect for others, as well as for the team and the firm, is another form of ethical leadership. Egalitarian treatment of their peers is essential; there is no favoritism and no bad treatment of any member of staff due to any sort of prejudice. Ethical leaders are capable of listening carefully, being sympathetic, fairly weighing opposing opinions, and equally appreciating their contributions.

Communication that is open

Being an effective communicator is also an indication of a moral leader. Being a good, open communicator is a skill that is often underestimated, from welcoming people to giving presentations and addressing subjects in meetings. Building an ethical team necessitates this communication trickling down into day-to-day talks, assisting in the development of trust and respect for one another.

Mediation that is fair

A fundamental asset of ethical leadership is the ability to mediate disputes. It is critical to be fair, to listen to all sides equally, and to find solutions that please both parties. Again, in building an egalitarian stance, the treatment of people is vital in an ethical leadership style.

Stress management that works

Ethical leaders must manage teams in which stress is an issue. These teams are often top performers that require consistent support and comprehension of the task at hand. One of the important characteristics of an ethical leader is the ability to manage difficult situations and to listen to the team carefully when things threaten to boil over. Being a soothing influence and cultivating an atmosphere of fairness and trust can assist with this.

Adapts to new situations

The capacity to listen to others and create shared solutions that benefit team members rather than just one individual is essential for ethical leadership. Change may be foisted upon a business, an environment, or a team without warning - or with warning. Understanding the changes, listening to concerns, but also making judgments that must be taken and respected throughout the team is what ethical leadership entails. Working in new locations and circumstances can occur at any time, and an ethical leader can assist in making the transition as seamless as possible.

There is no tolerance for ethical transgressions.

Ethical leaders hold themselves accountable on a regular basis, so doing the right thing at the right moment is critical - not when it is convenient or when someone is looking. This is why it is critical that individuals hold themselves accountable and do not enable others to violate ethical norms of behavior.

How can ethical leadership qualities emerge?

When you think about it, ethical leadership is quite straightforward. Ethical leadership is a method of placing people in positions of management and leadership who will "promote and be examples of appropriate, ethical conduct in their actions and relationships in the workplace." This may be characterized in the short and long term of a firm. In the near term, ethical leaders may increase morale and get employees enthused about their job while also making them satisfied with their management - going the additional mile to accomplish for the team. It may have a good impact on cooperation and general organization by making individuals feel glad to be there. Long-term ethical leadership can help to avoid organizational scandals, ethical quandaries, and ethical challenges. This may lead to greater partnerships and customers, which leads to more sales and profits, as well as the development of loyal workers, who are also an important component of a company's long-term success.

The good news is that you can create an ethical leadership

framework. It is completely attainable regardless of the size of your organization or the individuals that work for it. Here are a few examples of how you may improve your ethical leadership abilities:

- Deal with ethical quandaries as soon as possible.
- To minimize more problems, ensure that concerns are addressed and resolved as quickly as feasible.
- Pay attention to your stakeholders who are presenting concerns. Don't ignore them and try to escalate as soon as feasible.
- Consult your ethical framework – which may be a charter – to discover if the company has a disciplinary system in place.
- Improve your self-esteem.
- Dealing with ethically hard circumstances requires a lot of bravery and conviction to follow through on answers you believe are correct.
- Face the difficulties with honesty and confidence, no matter how difficult they may be.
- Don't be afraid to confront the issues.
- Understand the ethical hazards connected with certain processes.

Be aware of, act on, and handle ethical concerns concerning recruitment, termination, and promotion, among other things. while necessary, ethics and ethical legislation may need to be used in tandem to guarantee that you are not doing anything illegal even while following procedures that have been approved.

Education

Continue to educate yourself and other leaders on ethical business and management practices. Keep up to date on the current difficulties that employees may be encountering, whether they are related to specific cultures, faiths, or general issues.

Respect

Developing and garnering respect across teams and individuals within the organization.

Examples of ethical leadership

There are several real-world instances of ethical leadership in enterprises and institutions of all sizes. The first example comes from the United States, when, during a period of widespread governmental paralysis, one corporation chose to take a stand on the sale of guns in its stores. Dick's Sporting Goods chose to eliminate the option for consumers to buy weapons in their stores, much to the chagrin of some of their customers, but this was in response to mass shootings in schools and parks around the country. Despite initial criticism, Dicks Sporting Goods has recently delivered record earnings and share prices.

Procter & Gamble may have spent years pushing the frontiers of ethics, but a decision made in 2019 saw them confront a fundamental gender bias issue that they discovered throughout their organization. Their 'We See Equal' campaign encouraged them to look at recruiting in a new light, opening the door to more equal hiring processes and championing the inclusion of more women in key roles. "Leadership is about learning and teaching. Why waste getting old if you can't get wise? We have no mistakes here, we have learning moments," said Gary Ridge, CEO of WD40, in a Forbes interview. Ridge's ethical leadership standards have resulted in a 90% staff retention rate and a growth in shareholder value year after year over the previous 14 years.

Thomas has assisted organizations in developing more ethical leadership, such as Durban University Technical (DUT), where they assisted managers in grading the performance of their staff. The Thomas team eventually put up a mechanism that permitted the applicant to be treated and tested in a fair and ethical manner. Another outstanding example of ethical leadership comes from the outdoor apparel firm Patagonia, which has a strong ethical core owing to its founder, Yvon Chouinard. For many years, it has contributed at least 1% of sales or 10% of earnings to environmental organizations, whichever is greater. It's hardly surprising given that he invented mountain climbing. But when CFO Rose Marcario joined the firm in 2008 and became CEO in 2014, she pushed it to a whole new level. Marcario has battled to safeguard public lands and founded Patagonia Action Works to assist its clients in becoming active in environmental and social action. She has also urged clients to swap and mend existing garments rather than constantly buying new ones, according to the principle that "you do things not because it is convenient or when someone is watching, but because it is the right thing to do."

How do you cope with ethical difficulties at work?

What are the best methods for dealing with ethical difficulties at work? Here are a few examples of more typical procedures.

Clarification

Before making any decision, you should know all of the data from all sides. Make certain that you have a clear understanding of the situation, as well as the specifics. You want to be able to examine different opinions and backgrounds equally. Make sure you've considered cultural or linguistic differences and how they could play a role in the circumstance under investigation.

Make available resources and education.

It is possible that the ethical issue at hand requires further training and knowledge. One or more parties involved may require further knowledge on the ethics surrounding the specific issue. Providing ethics training may also create a precedent for team/company behavior. It also helps to teach the business on some of the less well-known aspects of ethics by encouraging individuals to discuss these topics more freely and to be more conscious of these difficulties in the future. In order to properly execute policy changes and create goals for senior leaders and managers, employers must provide educational opportunities for all employees. This might include literature or multimedia presentations explaining the significance of the changes, "icebreaker" games demonstrating appropriate behavior, or seminars with ethical experts.

If necessary, escalate the situation.

Once you've explained the problem with all parties, you should be able to go forward. However, you may discover that clarity isn't always sufficient. If it doesn't work, you'll need to escalate the matter, and you'll need to figure out who to notify next. This might be your boss's leadership, general counsel, a compliance officer, a hotline, an auditor, or an HR representative, depending on your organization.

Importantly, any ethical concerns that are not easily handled are escalated quickly, if required, and appropriate action is done.

Maintain consistency in dealing with comparable problems.

The most difficult challenge with ethical leadership is determining how consistent you should be in all of these judgments. The best method to clarify this is to develop a policy that outlines the ethics and ethical judgments that an organization must make. To that end, workers must sign the new policy, confirming their comprehension and vowing compliance. By doing so, they promise to hold themselves to a higher level and accept the penalties of failing to do so. Employers must agree to adhere to the same standard. The system will collapse if any party violates the agreement. Setting a precedent for how promptly and effectively comparable concerns are addressed is critical for fostering an ethical culture. Thomas can help you find and nurture ethical leaders.

Ethical leadership occurs when company executives act appropriately both within and outside of the office, in accordance with recognized principles and values. It's becoming clear that the future of business, and of driving change in our workplace practices, will be when we have more ethical leadership that aims to produce outcomes in a more holistic approach. From the extra rewards, including financial ones, to being accountable for acts and creating change that matters, ethical leadership is about being accountable for actions and promoting change that matters.

Emotional intelligence is sometimes the difference between an adequate and great leader. Leaders that are emotionally intelligent are self-aware, effective communicators, and can change their behavior to a range of scenarios. Thomas' Emotional Intelligence evaluation (also known as TEIQue) investigates emotional intelligence levels, fostering a climate of understanding that increases self-awareness among your leaders and may be used for both recruiting and training leaders.

CREATING A CULTURE OF ACCOUNTABILITY

Accountability is a decision. You may hold individuals accountable, but if they don't want to be held accountable, they will make excuses and refuse to accept responsibility. As a result, as a leader, you want to foster an environment in which people are naturally open, share their activities, commit to their goals, and make sound judgments. Instilling openness by coerced techniques and practices will result in a hostile and resistant culture. And resistive civilizations never carry out opposing strategic goals.

What exactly is an accountability culture?

A culture of accountability is one in which individuals are organically driven to own the outcomes of their activities and ambitions. It is a culture in which people are responsible and try to achieve their goals without the assistance of other influences. People in an accountable society accept responsibility for their actions (or lack thereof) but are assessed based on their decisions. For example, an employee may violate an organization's regulation in order to avoid escalating a conflict. In that case, it is more appropriate for leaders to determine whether the decision was proper rather than penalize the behavior without respect for the circumstances.

Why is it critical to foster an accountability culture?
Because it builds trust.

People who are accountable are trustworthy because they are predictable. When given a goal or a job, everyone understands they will either fulfill it or report their concerns as soon as possible. People abandon the victim attitude and take responsibility for the goals and measurements that have been assigned to them. Nobody likes to come up to a team meeting as the one who hasn't met their objective or has fallen far behind. People are more likely to meet the team's standards when they feel accountable to their supervisor and their coworkers. Instead of making up excuses, they accept their faults and hurdles. Their performance increases as a result. As a result, the team's performance increases. A culture of accountability compels people to report major roadblocks and difficulties early on in order to receive the assistance they require to overcome them. As a consequence, progress is made and there are no surprises when it is too late to deal with them. Execution is driven by an accountability culture.

How to Create an Accountability Culture

Transforming a culture by instilling the principle of responsibility in it. Change is difficult, let alone dramatic change. It takes a lot of effort, time, and dedication, but it is not impossible. Below are some ideas on how you might begin implementing change in your business. How-to-create-an-accountability-culture-infographic

1. Establish a safe atmosphere

Accountability necessitates trust. Your employees will not accept responsibility for their mistakes if they believe they are not allowed to fail. Permission to fail does not imply permission to labor less or be less careful. It is the recognition that your employees are human, that they make errors, and that certain situations are beyond their control. It is license to try new things, learn new things, and develop. Allowing your employees to make errors and move ahead helps them to be themselves, communicate their opinions and worries, and connect as human beings. Allow your employees to fail, to be themselves and vulnerable, so they will have the guts to seek assistance. Then you'll be able to provide your assistance and assist them in carrying out their obligations. Creating a secure workplace does not imply that individuals cannot fail, but rather that they do not feel threatened when they do.

2. Be accountable to your team, leaders.

Leaders must demonstrate that being vulnerable is acceptable. Leaders that never fail, never make errors, and never make mistakes develop teams that do the same. Leaders, like everyone else, are fallible and make errors. They transmit the message to their colleagues that they, too, may conceal and lie. They form groups that conceal and deceive. People imitate their leader's actions. The leader should take the initial step and model the conduct they want their followers to emulate. The team's leader must be the most trustworthy member. Their attitude then spreads to the rest of their squad.

However, the leader must have a method to "measure trust." That is difficult to achieve in any effective sense, but you can establish powerful indications. Here are a few examples of metrics to consider:

- How many people express reservations about the objective or project?
- How often do individuals seek assistance?
- How many times do individuals question the plan and the direction?
- In meetings, how frequently do individuals speak up?
- How often do people discuss their own troubles and difficulties?

Because each team and business has a unique culture, determining the best technique to assess whether your employees trust one another is not an easy task.

3. Establish clear expectations

Accountability is built on clarity in objectives, duties, and expectations. Someone cannot be held liable for something hazy. You can't just tell a salesperson to "make more sales" or a marketer to provide "more leads." That is insufficient. You must be more detailed. Encourage dedication to particular goals and KPIs by establishing clear expectations and aligning them with the team's goals and the company's strategy. To visualize and explain the relationship between personal objectives and your strategic strategy, use an online tool like Cascade. Set three tiers of goals, for example, for each team and individual:

Level of commitment

This is the person's basic minimal commitment. If you miss this goal more than once, it signifies you have a major problem that requires quick care.

Level of reality

This is the genuine goal for which the individual aspires. Missing it does not raise any warning signals, but it must be investigated in the proper context. Hitting it denotes a work well done that results in consistent progress.

Degree of excellence

When individuals achieve this goal, they are considered for a promotion. They do their duties well and above expectations, resulting in excellent outcomes.

4. Increase team transparency.

Share your own ambitions with the team. It fosters a transparent environment in which people are forced to be more open about their work and progress. Everyone is aware of what everyone else is doing. As a result, the team now holds the individual accountable. Nobody likes to let their teammates down. But here's the rub. Building business openness in a distrustful society has the opposite impact. People regard the initiative as yet another attempt to "catch them" when they do something wrong. Transparency produces more poison in a toxic culture. You must first create a trusting atmosphere before making it transparent.

5. Schedule review meetings

A habit of reporting on a regular basis benefits everyone concerned. On the one hand, teams and individuals are given the chance to discuss their progress, ask clarifying questions, request assistance, and illustrate what works and what does not. On the other side, management gains a clear picture of a project's development and performance, allowing them to correct course and provide assistance to those who require it. Not all of those gatherings require a rigid framework. Individual meetings work well with only a few questions, but team reporting meetings require more structure because you don't have time to go over every single project in depth. Use KPI templates to automate the process and decide what you'll report on before the meeting. Concentrate on "next steps" and handle every revelation that emerged from your talks. Finally, write down those pledges to ensure accountability. Specificity and frequent reporting make performance appraisals and accountability easier.

6. Empower your employees

Delegate power to them. Allow your employees to take the initiative and reward the desired behavior. Instead of having your employees send information up and wait for permission, give them the ability to make choices and address issues that they are most familiar with. Tell your employees to "ask for forgiveness, not permission." If your company's culture does not allow such a strong bottom-up approach, begin with tiny measures and work out the boundaries and power you may delegate incrementally. Although power can be backed by regulations and standards, people will continue to make mistakes. However, it is preferable to have handicapped staff than to make a few easily repairable blunders.

How leaders behave in an accountability culture

Accountability begins at the top. Making responsibility mandatory from the bottom creates a skeptical climate. So, how do accountable leaders conduct themselves? They never blame the team when something goes wrong. They accept full responsibility for the event or missed aim and, if given the opportunity, seek to correct it. Leaders with an empowered and accountable culture know that individuals truly want to do well in their roles and that when they don't, it's because they lack sufficient guidance. Whether it's more training, more context for their judgments, or more assistance. One fundamental reality is recognized by accountable leadership: They can claim credit for everything their team accomplishes correctly as long as they accept complete accountability for everything their team does incorrectly.

A leader is responsible to both their management and their team. As a result, if a team fails to complete its project on time, its leaders should hold themselves accountable to the team for failing to provide adequate assistance to achieve the deadline. If a team member degrades their team's performance, it is the leader who is held accountable to their management, not the underperforming individual. This approach changes the focus to finding a solution that addresses the source of the problem. Perhaps the team member is overburdened, lacks experience and training, or is better suited for a different job. In any event, accountable leaders avoid pointing fingers.

How to make accountability a core part of your workplace culture.

It is hard to build a high-performing team when there is no responsibility.

Why?
Simply put, when no one takes responsibility for making choices, addressing concerns, and fixing problems, nothing gets done.

Accountability occurs when individuals accept responsibility for their own acts. It is about taking the initiative and understanding that individuals not only have the ability to cause issues, but also to solve them. In this chapter, we'll look at what responsibility looks like at work, why it's important, and how to incorporate it into your company culture:

What does workplace responsibility entail?

In the workplace, accountability implies that all workers are accountable for their actions, behaviors, performance, and choices. It is also associated to increased job dedication and staff morale, which leads to improved performance. Recognizing that the outcomes of your work affect the success of other team members and the overall performance of the firm. When workers are held accountable, they accept responsibility for their actions and do not assume it is someone else's obligation. It is essentially the inverse of passing the buck. The person who is personally accountable Apple's notion of the directly responsible individual (DRI) is a prime illustration of workplace responsibility. At Apple, everything, large or little, is allocated to someone who is personally accountable for it. DRIs are held responsible for the success or failure of the projects to which they are assigned. There is less potential for transferring blame and greater clarity regarding who makes choices when responsibility is expressly assigned.

Trust is built when team members constantly display ownership and accountability. As a consequence, there is less micromanagement and improved performance.

What happens at work when there is a lack of accountability?

Simply put, a lack of responsibility harms the team. When people are not held accountable, the delay of one person becomes the delay of the entire team. One shortage snowball into larger ones. When missed deadlines, tardiness, and incomplete work are allowed, they tend to become the norm. People learn that the true deadline is a week later than the reported one, that being 10 minutes late for meetings is OK, and that mediocre work is acceptable. Your team suffers, and as a result, your workplace culture suffers as well. Accountability is lacking.

When a team member fails to meet their promises and is not held accountable, the remainder of the team becomes frustrated and disengaged. A lack of responsibility in the workplace, according to Partners in Leadership, results in:

- Team morale is low.
- Priorities are unclear among the squad.
- Employee disengagement Unmet team and individual goals
- Low trust levels High turnover

How do you demonstrate accountability at work?

There is clearly a significant penalty for a lack of responsibility. So, how can you prevent or correct the situation? Before you can think about how to incorporate responsibility into your workplace culture, you must first look within. Do you hold yourself accountable at work? Starting with goals and expectations is a smart place to start. You can't be accountable if you don't know what you're accountable for. Set clear and quantifiable objectives for yourself and your team so that everyone, including you, understands what you're attempting to accomplish.

Following that, you should address the gap between expectations and performance. You may close the gap between what you're doing and what you're meant to be doing after you grasp your goals and expectations. Is there an abyss where items go missing because you didn't notice they landed on your plate? And most crucially, accept accountability for your actions. When you admit you've made a mistake, you also admit you have the ability to correct it. That is the allure of accountability. Examples of how to demonstrate your personal accountability at work:

- Complete the duties that have been allocated to you by the agreed-upon deadline.
- Take responsibility for your team's success and make an effort to assist your team when necessary.
- When scheduling meetings, respect everyone's time by arriving prepared and on time (and expect others to do the

same).

- Take responsibility for the issues you raise by bringing solutions to the table.
- Don't brush problems under the rug or believe they've already been resolved. Instead, raise concerns as they emerge.

How to make responsibility a fundamental value of your team and a key element of your culture

We reject holding people accountable because we are uncomfortable doing so, we forget to do so, or we are unsure how to do so. Here's how you address these concerns and foster an accountability culture in the workplace.

1. Set a good example by holding yourself accountable first.

As previously said, as a manager, you create the tone, performance, and culture for your team. People will take your lead. If you consistently arrive late for meetings, miss deadlines, and refuse to admit mistakes, the team will do the same.

2. Establish team objectives

Setting objectives is an important component of developing an accountability culture on your team. It helps to clarify what you're attempting to accomplish together. But keep in mind that not all objectives are created equal. Goals that foster responsibility must be quantifiable, explicit, and difficult. The OKR framework (objective and key results) is our preferred method for setting objectives. The beauty of OKRs is that they are not imposed from on high. They are readily trackable and are created as a team. Furthermore, they should be linked to wider organizational goals so that everyone understands their influence on the big picture. This helps everyone understand their duties and what is expected of them on an individual and team level.

3. Improve your feedback abilities using the OKR framework

Giving difficult criticism is difficult, but it is a talent that can be honed. Giving feedback is one of the most essential things you can do as a manager. When you offer feedback on a regular basis (including good feedback), it becomes much simpler to deliver difficult comments. It also lowers the possibility that your direct report would be startled by the comments they get, leading to additional alienation.

Effective feedback is made up of several components:

- Ensure psychological safety: It is critical to provide negative feedback in a secure, private setting, such as one-on-one discussions. But keep in mind that psychological safety does not develop overnight. Work with your team members to establish a safe atmosphere where they can be vulnerable and themselves. If they don't, it will be far more difficult for them to accept your input.

- Assume good intentions: Effective feedback stems from a genuine desire to assist someone in growing. You must 'give a damn.' Assume that the issue you're addressing was not done maliciously. It all boils down to having one another's backs.

- Please be specific: When you're overly generic, you're not helping your team member. Use a particular example to back up your suggestions; this will help them realize how to improve. Check out this list of constructive feedback examples for more information on how to offer effective constructive feedback.

4. Establish a feedback culture.

It's not only about being able to offer good criticism; it's also about being open to accepting it and making room for it. When you do not cultivate a culture of two-way feedback and your team members do not feel comfortable to speak out, they begin to disconnect. Vital Smarts conducted a study of over 800 experts and discovered:

- 52% are hesitant to share peer performance issues such as inappropriate shortcuts, inadequate attention to detail, and unfinished work.

- 47% said they are hesitant to express concerns or suggestions that might enhance a business aspect because it encroaches on someone else's territory.

- When policy actions begin to have unanticipated negative impacts, 49% wait more than a week before speaking up.

- When they feel someone (or a group) has made a poor strategic decision, 55% are hesitant to disclose it.

That's a lot of missed opportunities and resources being squandered. Encourage two-way feedback so that your staff feels comfortable discovering and expressing concerns. Make the lettuce contract with your team to promote feedback.

5. Establish responsibility as a habit.

Setting a reminder to provide and ask feedback as part of the agenda for each meeting can assist ensure that input flows regularly. We feel that one-on-ones and team sessions are excellent venues for developing an accountability habit.

Here are a few meeting questions that individuals add to their one-on-one agendas to make responsibility a habit:

- Is there anything we should get started on as a group?
- Do you want me to give you more or less direction on your work?
- Do you believe you are receiving adequate feedback on your work? If not, where would you want further information?
- Is there an element of your profession that you would want further assistance or coaching with?
- How could we enhance the way our team collaborates?

6. Maintain a record of your promises and hold each other responsible.

If you vow to give more feedback to your direct reports, make it a future agenda item to hold yourself responsible. If an employee agrees to provide a work back schedule for a project by a specific day, make sure you have a mechanism to check in on that day. Making sure you assign action items during meetings is an easy approach to build a culture of responsibility - or, if the harm has already been done, remedy a lack of accountability. This is an excellent method for holding each member of your team accountable for their behavior

7. Use an accountability framework

In most cases, a lack of responsibility is unintentional. It is frequently the outcome of several issues, one of which being unclear roles and duties. Accountability is practically difficult when there is a lack of clarity about who is responsible for what. In reality, according to a Gallup poll, just half of employees firmly believe they know what is expected of them at work. Fortunately, accountability frameworks such as the RACI matrix can assist with this issue. This accountability structure, also known as a RACI chart, guarantees that everyone working in a project is allocated a responsibility at all times. These functions are divided into four degrees of accountability:

- Those who are accountable for finishing the work at hand.
- Accountable: Those who are ultimately responsible for the job or deliverable's fulfillment. This person is also in charge of allocating work to others who are in charge of finishing it.
- These people are often the subject-matter experts on the topic at hand. They are participating in the project's specific stage as consultants and advisors.
- Informed: These are the people who are brought up to speed on the project's development at each step. This is often done through one-way communication.

The following is an example of a RACI matrix for an engineering team Example of a RACI Chart for an Engineering Team. Holding coworkers responsible is an added bonus. Creating an accountability culture on your immediate staff is one tale. Another is to hold your peers responsible. How do you keep your coworkers accountable so that you may improve how you collaborate throughout the organization? Holding your teammates accountable, contrary to common assumption, does not include pointing fingers or assigning blame. It all comes down to mutual support. Here are some crucial considerations for increasing accountability among your coworkers:

Transparency is being open and honest with your coworkers. We may keep our cards close to our chests owing to complex workplace dynamics or operating in isolation. However, being transparent fosters accountability, both for yourself and your colleagues.

Help one another: Working in silos quickly breeds a lack of accountability for anything that happens outside of your team. However, an organization is a jigsaw, and each team is a component of the overall image. To reach your company's objectives, you must collaborate. Even if it's 'outside of your job description,' explore how you can help each other. Their troubles are also your problems.

Don't overlook peer-to-peer one-on-ones: One-on-one meetings are much too frequently designated for manager/direct report interactions. Peer-to-peer one-on-ones, on the other hand, are a crucial aspect in fostering empathy and accountability throughout the company. It's simple to blame another team for a project gone bad. However, by engaging with your colleagues through frequent meetings, you may better grasp roadblocks and restrictions and have a deeper understanding of team choices. Overall, building an accountability culture on your team will not only enhance employee morale and productivity, but it will also provide your team with the autonomy and feeling of ownership they require to fully thrive. If you believe your team lacks responsibility, it's time to make some changes!

Fostering open communication workplace

Employees who feel heard and respected are more likely to stay with their firm and are nearly five times more likely to feel empowered to achieve their best job. However, fostering open communication in the workplace is not as straightforward as it may appear. These five useful hints will assist SMB employers in developing or revising their office communication strategy. Employees that are happy and engaged are the foundation of any successful firm. One of the most effective strategies to increase employee satisfaction is to guarantee that their problems, ideas, and views are acknowledged. However, all too frequently, this is disregarded by the organization's administration. An open communication environment is one in which people can freely communicate their views and ideas to one another. Having an open communication-centered business culture can result in various organizational benefits:

Higher employee engagement: When employees feel comfortable discussing their opinions, they are more likely to engage with their employers, which may deepen their commitment to the firm and lead to higher productivity.

Increased diversity, equity, and inclusion: Everyone has the right to be heard. Encouraging employees to speak out and share their ideas makes more individuals feel involved and makes them more inclined to provide constructive feedback. It also assists employees in developing trust with their organization, which nearly two-thirds of workers think has a direct influence on their sense of belonging at work.

Higher levels of productivity: When employees feel

appreciated and respected, they are more driven. According to study, folks who feel heard on the workplace are 4.6 times more likely to be empowered to accomplish their best work.

In contrast, failing to maintain an open channel of communication in the office can have a detrimental impact on a company. Low morale, unfavorable reviews on sites like Glassdoor (which can harm a company's reputation), and, finally, staff loss are some of the consequences of not providing employees with a means of communication.

5 methods to promote open communication in the workplace

Fortunately, creating a plan to encourage employees to speak up is not as tough as one may imagine. Here are five suggestions for encouraging open communication in the workplace.

1. Be truthful, polite, and invested in the goals of your staff.

Everyone engaging in open communication must be truthful. Business executives should ensure that all business communications maintain the greatest levels of respect, and that workers understand that this is also required of them. If someone signals otherwise, remind them that their input is valuable but must be offered politely. This is an important step in fostering open communication in the workplace. Understanding and emphasizing the goals of employees is another method to demonstrate respect. When people join a firm, they frequently learn about its goal, values, and vision. However, it is typically a one-sided discussion in which employees' aims and desires are not expressed. Understanding team members' goals allows leaders to adapt learning and development to maximize value for workers and the company. Developing a mentoring program and promoting involvement may also assist guarantee that their career goals are reached, providing mentors with the opportunity to expand their managerial abilities, and even have a beneficial influence on corporate revenues.

2. Check in on a regular basis

Over half of employees wish their employers polled them more frequently, and a weekly, one-question survey designed to give anonymous feedback can assist managers in staying in contact with their staff. Organizations can utilize a low-cost survey system or a performance management platform with surveying features to ask employees a new question each week and report the results to management for assessment. This will assist corporate executives in addressing employee complaints before they become a larger problem. To fully reap the advantages of surveys, organizations must ensure that they are effectively administered. Business executives should deliberate how they will create and conduct an employee survey, evaluate the data, and build an action plan based on the results when creating one.

3. Request anonymous ideas.

In addition to sending out surveys, providing a permanent, judgment-free space for employees to voice their thoughts might be beneficial. Companies should think about adopting an online suggestion box system that allows employees to provide anonymous comments and suggestions. This informs employees that they have the authority to suggest ways to enhance their workplace. It may also motivate them to bring to management's notice issues with which they are not normally comfortable dealing.

4. Respond to feedback

It is vital to respond to employee input in order to preserve open communication in the workplace. After all, communication is a two-way street, and your corporate culture depends on employees thinking they are heard. Business executives should put in place a method to acknowledge and process all comments. Discussing poll results at company-wide town halls or team-specific meetings might be part of this. Every suggestion does not have to result in change, but it should be acknowledged and taken into account. Employees will be more likely to contribute to the open communication culture as a result of this. When your organization allows free communication, you might be amazed at how many intelligent comments and suggestions you'll receive. Some of the recommendations will almost certainly be unfavorable. Business leaders must remember to notice and resolve such issues, as well as recognize the need of having a framework in place for employees to convey their ideas.

5. Evaluate the success of your open communication strategy.

Asking for and reading feedback isn't enough to establish that you've effectively built an open culture or to find areas for improvement. To do so, you must gather and evaluate relevant qualitative and quantitative data. The Society of Human Resource Management (SHRM) suggests the following data points for corporate leaders to consider measuring: Qualitative data, including anecdotal evidence of improvements in employee perceptions and attitudes following the implementation of an open communication approach

Quantitative statistics such as attrition, productivity, and employee satisfaction rates A partner to assist you in promoting open communication Small company owners are busy and focused on expansion, so having an independent third-party agency weigh in on or assist create your communication efforts may be quite beneficial. ExtensisHR, a professional employer organization (PEO), can handle all of this and more. ExtensisHR, for example, in addition to complete human resources, employee benefits, and risk and compliance services, provides the following:

HR professionals to help small firms build open communication plans, mentorship programs, and employee survey tactics.

Access to 15Five, a premier performance management software that enables engagement surveys, feedback collection, weekly employee check-ins, one-on-one meetings, performance trend monitoring, and more, for an affordable price.

A strong learning and development knowledge base including training themes such as communication, teamwork, team building, and dealing with disengagement.

The importance of open communication in the workplace

What are the benefits of open communication in the workplace?

Your company's lifeblood is open communication. In its absence, no internal system can function properly. Consider a workplace where various departments and teams are separated by silos. When no one communicates freely, two persons may wind up working on the same assignment, and some projects may be abandoned since no one completed them. Open communication not only prevents such difficulties, but also propels your company's growth to new heights. And it accomplishes this in the following manner. Employee contentment is increased by open communication. Employee satisfaction is one of the most important goals for every company. It should be, because happy employees are 20% more productive than dissatisfied employees. Furthermore, they are less likely to leave your organization, saving you thousands of dollars in new talent acquisition costs. Open communication is essential for keeping employees pleased. Atlassian discovered in a study of over 1000 employees that employees who receive honest feedback, personal transparency, and mutual respect are 80% more likely to express great emotional well-being. Open communication contributes to workplace satisfaction.

Atlassian provided the image.

Open communication bridges cultural divides and fosters inclusivity.

Many years ago, one of the employees on a team I was leading abruptly resigned. He'd begun four months before, at a significant pay raise from his former position. Nobody had noticed any signs of dissatisfaction. When asked why, he stated, "I don't feel like I belong here." Unfortunately, such occurrences are more prevalent than you may believe. Most big firms nowadays have a diverse staff comprised of people from many cultures. While this promotes creativity and innovation in your business, it may also make individuals feel unwelcome and out of place. Religion, clothes, food, language, music, professional behavior, and other factors comprise culture, according to anthropologist Cristina De Rossi. As a result, when people from different cultures collaborate on shared goals, these factors might create hurdles to cooperation and productivity. Not to mention concerns like lost cash sources and public relations disasters. Creating an inclusive culture is therefore critical for engaging and retaining people. And the good news is that your staff can overcome these hurdles via cultural awareness, education, and understanding – all of which are characteristics of open communication.

Open communication bridges cultural divides. Employees may ask clarifying questions and communicate their problems openly, even if it makes them vulnerable. When people perceive that it is OK to be vulnerable, they are more inclined to work across cultural barriers. In this approach, open communication assists workers in getting over the uncertainty and misconceptions produced by cultural differences, and everyone feels like they're on the same team. Employee engagement rises with open communication. According to research, highly engaged employees are 17% more productive than their counterparts. These are employees that work hard and go above and beyond in their jobs. When you promote open communication, you show that you are eager to listen to your employees' issues and suggestions. As a result, you establish yourself as a caring and trustworthy employer. Open communication should be a tool in your employee engagement efforts if it isn't already. Allowing workers to openly express their emotions and opinions engages them more and strengthens their dedication to your firm.

Productivity is increased via open communication.You can have a well-trained and talented workforce, but it will be worthless if there is minimal production. And if your employees are unable to properly interact with one another, they will be unable to complete tasks. As previously said, open communication enhances engagement, and engagement leads to increased productivity. But it doesn't mean it doesn't have an effect on productivity. Communication is more successful when people are open. Your workers receive the appropriate information at the appropriate moment. Furthermore, efficient communication can boost workplace productivity by 25%.

Open communication helps to clarify expectations.The first need for your staff to thrive in their professions is to understand exactly what has to be done and why. Meeting corporate objectives requires providing required instructions and outlining each worker's responsibility. Open communication provides a clear roadmap for work. You'll be setting them up for failure even before they start if you don't set clear expectations. And what assists you in setting clear expectations? Communication that is open. In reality, it not only leads to a better comprehension of responsibilities, but it also holds employees accountable. By publicly sharing goals and key performance indicators, you reinforce their significance and provide employees with a benchmark to strive toward.

Open communication improves psychological security. Repressing concerns in the workplace simply exacerbates them. The sooner you can stop them, the better for everyone. Let's imagine your team members believe you don't take their workloads into account when allocating new duties. As a result, their dislike of you is building. And if they are not permitted to express their concerns freely, they are more likely to burn out or resign. As a result, workers must feel comfortable in expressing their thoughts. They should not be condemned, blamed, or penalized in any manner. As a result, psychological safety is a significant motivator of employee engagement. When a culture of openly discussing one's opinions and feelings is established, employees understand that it is safe to do so without fear. This fosters a climate in which employees are neither afraid to provide honest criticism, nor are they outraged when such feedback is provided to them. Similarly, executives are more open to proposals that might help the company improve and reach its full potential.

Open communication improves team camaraderie. Employees are more aware of one another's preferences, communication styles, obstacles, and even weaknesses when they communicate openly. When done correctly, it also demonstrates to them that their peers appreciate and respect them for who they are and what they provide to the team. What was the end result? Relationships get stronger as trust grows. What company wouldn't want it as part of their employee experience strategy?

Open communication strengthens team ties. Closed communication, on the other hand, makes people appear deceptive, manipulative, critical, and scary. Employees construct emotional walls to defend themselves in response. As a result, staff engagement and retention suffer. Communication that is open encourages creativity and innovation. According to 250 academics from 60 different universities, creativity is the most important 21st century ability. Because open communication enables team members to share their ideas, they may build on one another's ideas to come up with creative solutions to challenges. By accepting their ideas and comments, you can demonstrate to employees that you rely on them to solve problems and build the firm. This allows employees to perceive themselves as a vital part of the business and fosters a deeper feeling of ownership.

The Three Foundations of Open Communication

Open communication may appear to be simple to grasp and

implement. However, contrary to common assumption, it is not about being brutally honest and not caring about the sentiments of your coworkers. In reality, the reverse is true. However, many leaders do things in the name of open communication that end up destroying it. The concepts outlined below will assist you in getting it properly.

Egolessness

If you and your team members are unable to keep your egos in control, open communication may appear to be threatening. You must set a good example for your team to follow. After all, when communication is open and two-way, your staff may query, give advice, or express their feelings about how you have been doing things thus far. As a leader, you should have the maturity and spirit to support such conduct rather than becoming offended by it. Trust Business literature is replete with the appropriate words and phrases to use when providing feedback to employees. But it's not so much about the words as it is about the workers' faith in you. When there is no confidence that you are looking out for the best interests of your team members, even the most favorable comments might be detrimental. When people trust you, however, even the most critical input is understood and valued.

Training

It is critical to demonstrate to your staff how to properly utilize open communication in the workplace. Managers and workers alike must learn to speak honestly and encourage others to do the same. As a result, having a structured communication training program in place is critical. Teamwork is required to move your staff ahead toward a common objective. This is because when people pool their own talents and abilities with those of others, they achieve far more than they would have done alone. However, collaboration presents some distinct obstacles. The distinctions that enable us to contribute to the team can present hurdles to good collaboration with others. As this essay demonstrates, open communication goes a long way toward removing these obstacles and enabling quick and simple access to critical information. So consider these aspects and consider how you may implement the ideas we discussed in your business. Also, bear in mind that the greatest employee engagement technologies may help you accelerate your efforts to create an open communication culture.

SETTING AND ACHIEVING GOALS

Goal setting and achievement are critical components of good leadership. The SMART criteria give a systematic framework for leaders and teams to express and achieve goals with clarity and accuracy. Specific, Measurable, Achievable, Relevant, and Time-bound is an acronym that stands for Specific, Measurable, Achievable, Relevant, and Time-bound. We will go into the relevance of SMART objectives in leadership, the different components of the SMART framework, and how leaders may adopt this strategy for best results in this detailed investigation. Leadership entails directing a group toward a unified vision, and goal-setting is crucial to this process. SMART objectives greatly contribute to the success of leaders and their teams by offering a clear path and establishing an accountability culture.

1. Detail and Clarity:
The "S" in SMART stands for Specific, highlighting the need of specificity in goal setting. Leaders must clearly define their goals, leaving no space for misunderstanding. Specific goals provide the team a clear direction, avoiding misunderstandings and increasing productivity.

2. Accountability and Measurability:
The letter "M" in SMART stands for Measurable objectives. Leaders must establish metrics or indications of growth and success. Measurable objectives allow teams to track their progress, instilling a feeling of accountability in team members. Quantifiable outcomes give real proof of progress, inspiring people to continue on track.

3. Achievability and Realistic Expectations:
Achievable is represented by the letter "A" in SMART. Leaders must develop objectives that are reasonable and attainable within the limits and resources available. Setting unrealistic objectives, while admirable, can lead to dissatisfaction and demotivation. Achievable goals push people to expand their talents without overwhelming them.

4. Alignment and relevance:

The letter "R" in SMART stands for Relevant goals. Leaders must verify that the goals are consistent with the organization's overarching purpose and objectives. Relevant goals contribute to the wider mission, increasing team members' feeling of significance and participation. Aligning objectives with organizational strategy ensures that efforts are focused on the most significant outcomes.

5. Time constraint and urgency:

The "T" in SMART highlights the importance of setting time-bound goals. Leaders must establish deadlines in order to instill a feeling of urgency and commitment. Time-bound goals assist to prioritize efforts and reduce procrastination. Setting deadlines also enables for the assessment of work at regular intervals, allowing for timely modifications and improvements.

How to Use SMART Goals in Leadership:

Now that we've established the importance of SMART objectives, let's look at how leaders may put them into action:

1. Setting Collaborative Goals:

In order to achieve collective ownership and commitment, involve team members in the goal-setting process. Collaborative goal-setting leverages the team's different viewpoints and experience, making the objectives more robust and feasible.

2. Continuous Monitoring and Evaluation:

Create a mechanism for tracking and evaluating progress on a regular basis. Tracking key performance indicators, evaluating milestones, and finding changes from the original plan are all part of this process. Leaders may give timely feedback and assistance by checking in on a regular basis.

3. Adaptability and adaptability:

While SMART objectives give a structure, leaders must stay adaptive and open to changes. External causes, changing circumstances, or new knowledge may force changes to the initial objectives. Leaders must foster flexibility while retaining overarching direction.

4. Transparency and communication:

The successful implementation of SMART objectives requires effective communication. Leaders must clearly define their objectives, the reasons behind them, and the expected outcomes. Transparent communication builds confidence among team members and develops a shared knowledge of the group's goals.

5. Acknowledgement and Celebration:

Recognize and appreciate both large and little accomplishments. Recognition encourages excellent actions and pushes people to keep working. Celebrating accomplishments helps to foster a healthy team culture and encourages continuing dedication to the established goals.

Difficulties and Considerations:

While SMART objectives are a valuable tool, leaders should be aware of potential problems and take the following things into account when implementing them:

1. Balancing Short-Term and Long-Term Objectives:

Leaders must create a balance between short-term goals for immediate development and long-term goals that match with the strategic vision of the firm. This balance keeps the team focused on both current objectives and long-term goals.

2. Avoid Putting Too Much Emphasis on Metrics:

While quantifiable results are important, leaders should avoid focusing solely on quantitative measurements. Qualitative factors like as team cooperation, creativity, and employee happiness are also critical for long-term success.

3. Providing Appropriate Resources:

Leaders must ensure that teams have the resources they need, such as time, money, and labor, to fulfill their objectives. Inadequate resources might stymie development and cause team members to get frustrated.

4. Goal Alignment Monitoring:

As organizational priorities shift, executives must examine whether existing goals are still in line with the broader strategic direction. Changes may be required to maintain relevance and effectiveness.

SMART objectives are an essential component of good leadership because they provide a methodical approach to goal-setting that improves clarity, responsibility, and outcomes. Individuals may steer their teams to success with precision and purpose by implementing the SMART criteria into their leadership techniques. Leaders that use the SMART framework enable their teams to overcome obstacles, adapt to change, and create meaningful outcomes that benefit both individual and organizational growth.

10 SMART Leadership Development Goals

Having specified, measurable, attainable, relevant, and time-bound (SMART) goals encourages leaders to concentrate on tactics for improving their leadership abilities. Individuals and organizations may construct a clear path for reaching their intended results and driving continuous progress in their leadership practices by defining SMART goals for leadership development. We've put up a handy list of 10 SMART goals with examples for leadership development and developing a strong and productive team.

1. Improve Communication Capabilities

Communication is one of the most crucial abilities to develop in the workplace in order to foster a culture of transparency. For example, you may take a brief communication course once a month for six months. After six months, solicit feedback from team members and management, and build future course subjects on their responses.

This SMART objective is broken down as follows:

- Every month, complete a specialized communication course based on feedback.
- quantifiable: Completing one course every month for six months is the quantifiable portion.
- Achievable: Set a date and time to finish each course.
- Relevant: Effective communication may assist leaders in developing strong team connections and minimizing

misunderstandings.
- The target will be completed in six months.

2. Recognize and Accept Constructive Criticism

Learning how to cope with and accept constructive criticism as part of becoming a better leader demonstrates humility and openness to learning. Start seeing constructive criticism, for example, as a chance to progress. For three months, you may keep note of what your team said and how you reacted to it.

This is a SMART objective because:

- To be more specific, begin viewing constructive criticism as a chance to learn and improve.
- Track the times when you take constructive criticism without becoming defensive. Take note of what was mentioned as feedback and how you responded.
- Achievable: You may accomplish this objective by maintaining a physical or online tracker on hand to record constructive feedback received during the next four months.
- Accepting constructive criticism is an important leadership ability that will benefit you and your team.
- You have three months to practice this talent.

3. Master the Art of Giving Constructive Feedback

You may learn to provide constructive feedback to your team now that you are more comfortable taking constructive criticism. As an example, attempt to deliver constructive comments in a courteous manner. Track instances when you offered high-quality, relevant input during the next quarter. Each month, get feedback from your team on your efforts and, if required, re-evaluate.

This sample fits the SMART objective requirements as follows:

- Provide constructive feedback to your team members in a timely and appropriate manner.

- Measurable: Keep track of the times you provided constructive criticism to team members, what you said, and how you felt. Each month, solicit feedback on your efforts.
- Achievable: Achieve this objective by planning ahead of time for each session.
- Constructive comments may assist team members in identifying areas for growth and build a culture of accountability, constant learning, and progress.
- Time-bound: Put this expertise to the test during the next three months.
- Create Connections with Your Team

4. Foster Relationships Among Members of Your Team

Relationships with team members can help to foster a supportive and engaging atmosphere. You may, for example, schedule monthly check-ins with each employee to discuss projects and general career concerns. After three months, solicit feedback on the check-ins and revise the approach as needed.

This SMART goal example is broken down as follows:

- Specific: The idea is to meet with each team member once a month in a casual atmosphere to get to know them.
- quantifiable: Having monthly check-ins for three months is the quantifiable aspect.
- Achievable: It's doable if you set aside 30 minutes a few times a month.
- Building great relationships with your team members is necessary for creating a positive work atmosphere and increasing productivity.
- The target will be completed in three months.

5. Be More Open to Change

Leaders may instill confidence and trust in their team members by having the ability to adapt to change. As an example, you may finish a change management training course and then use what you've learned over the next six months. During this time, keep track of times where you quickly adapted to unforeseen changes.

This is a SMART objective because:

- Complete a change management course and use what you learn in the workplace.
- Measurable: After completing the course, keep track of occasions where you effectively coped with unexpected workplace changes.
- Achievable: Reach this objective by investing in a practical course that includes directions or tools for putting the knowledge into action. The course should have a finish date.
- Relevant: Adaptability may assist leaders in being nimble and resilient in the face of unanticipated problems.
- Time-bound: Achieve this target in six months while always looking for methods to improve adaptability in various circumstances.

6. Hold Successful Meetings

A simple email might sometimes replace a meeting, yet meetings remain an important aspect of the business. One approach to do this is to use a meeting calendar over the following two months to develop your meeting and presentation abilities. Allow team members to offer comments and iterate as necessary.

This sample fits the SMART objective requirements as follows:

- Improve your meeting and presentation abilities in particular.
- Measurable actions include maintaining meetings within your team's schedule and keeping note of whether they run over or under the time estimate.
- Achievable: To keep team members informed, plan and distribute the meeting schedule and agenda.
- Relevant: Meetings that are efficient save time and keep everyone focused on their duties, allowing you to communicate more effectively.

- Time-bound: Spend two months working on this aim.

7. Encourage the Use of Knowledge-Sharing Systems

You must have mechanisms in place for sharing information and resources if you want your team to function successfully and efficiently. For example, you may create a repository of standard operating procedures (SOPs) for your team's processes. After three months, assess how frequently team members seek direct support and revise SOPs as necessary.

The SMART requirements for this objective are listed below:

- Create a centralized repository for your team's SOPs.
- Measurable: Once the hub is operational, keep track of how frequently team members seek direct support and alter SOPs as needed.
- Achievable: This may be accomplished by identifying the procedures and developing a shared SOP hub in a set timeframe, such as one quarter.
- Relevant: A leader may produce a better skilled team by encouraging professional development and giving chances for skill development.
- Time-bound: Over the following three months, launch this project and teach everyone on the SOPs.

8. cultivate Internal Talent:

A leader who strives to cultivate internal talent may foster a culture of learning and development inside the organization. For example, you may hold talent development seminars or mentoring programs every three months for a year and analyze how many team members attend each one.

Use this SMART goal example to develop internal talent:

- Implement team-wide talent development seminars or mentoring programs.
- Measurable: Keep track of how many team members attend each of these sessions.

- Achievable: Spend time looking for relevant workshops and making them available to your staff.
- Relevant: Developing internal talent aids in the retention of high-performing employees while expanding the company's talent pool.
- Time-bound: Achieve this objective within the next year by seeking for professional development tools and chances.

9. Express gratitude and recognition

Recognizing and appreciating team members entails providing positive comments on their efforts and successes. Plan a fun monthly team event to demonstrate your thanks for your team members. After six months, solicit feedback and revise as required.

The SMART goal example is as follows:

- Plan exciting activities to demonstrate your thanks to your staff.
- quantifiable: Having monthly events for six months and asking your members for comments on the experience is the quantifiable aspect.
- Achievable: It is feasible by allocating a corporate budget and organizing a monthly fun event.
- Appreciation and acknowledgment may empower team members while also improving morale and motivation.
- Time-bound: Complete this task in six months.

10. Become at Ease with Task Delegation

Trusting your team members and delegating power over activities and projects while you are away helping you to concentrate on higher-level duties. over example, you can begin outsourcing duties without feeling compelled to micromanage over the following six months. Following that, get input from your team.

This sample fits the SMART objective requirements as follows:

- Delegate duties to team members with confidence.

- Measurable: Keep track of how many tasks you assign and their success rate. Take note of how comfortable your team members are with taking on assigned tasks.
- Achievable: Set aside time each week to allocate and track each member's accomplishment of these duties.
- Relevant: Leaders may establish responsibility and offer opportunity for team members to learn new skills and knowledge by instilling trust and confidence in them.
- Time-bound: Achieve this in six months by properly dispersing employment.

Exude Human Capital Can Help You Become a Better Leader Exude Human Capital Can Help You Become a Better Leader. Setting SMART objectives for leadership development is critical to becoming an effective and successful leader. Leadership coaching can help you gain momentum toward your goals. Exude is a consultancy organization that has assisted businesses in implementing leadership and staff development skills. We want to provide you with exceptional advice on building competent leaders to advance the mission of your firm. Our objective is to assist you. Learn more about our leadership development program or get in touch with us right now.

Five Things Holding You Back from Reaching Your Goals

Setting and achieving objectives is an important step toward personal growth and accomplishment. Goals, whether career-related, health-related, or personal development-focused, give a road map to achievement. Nonetheless, despite our best efforts, many of us fall short of our objectives. In this chapter, we will look at five frequent issues that prevent people from accomplishing their goals. You may unleash your full potential and drive yourself to success by knowing these hurdles and adopting tactics to overcome them.

Obstacles to Achieving Your Objectives

1. Fear of failure

Fear of failing is one of the most major impediments to achieving our objectives. It's normal to be concerned about the unknown and potential setbacks or disappointments. Allowing fear to immobilize us, on the other hand, might hinder us from taking the required risks and grasping chances that lead to success. To achieve your objectives, you must confront your fears of failure at some time, or you will likely never make any progress at all. To overcome your fear of failure, attempt to redefine your mental image of failure. Try changing your perspective and viewing failure as a stepping stone to learning and progress. This will assist you in accepting the lessons that failure provides so that you may utilize them as fuel to continue on your path toward your objectives. To achieve your objectives, you must be willing to fail. Failure is a natural part of the process.

2. Inconsistency

Without a clear picture of what we want to achieve, our objectives become hazy and illusive. Lack of clarity makes it harder to design a plan or practical measures to achieve your goals. You empower yourself to take deliberate action and make real progress toward your final goal by acquiring clarity about what you want to achieve. Defining your goals with detail might assist you in gaining clarity. That means you should be as detailed as possible when creating your objectives, including information like how you will assess your progress and the date you want to attain your final goal. Setting a time limit helps to guarantee that you stay on track and don't procrastinate along the way. And speaking of which...

3. Disorganization

Procrastination is a quiet dream killer that almost everyone encounters at some time in their lives. As someone who constantly issues with procrastination, I understand how easy it is to become engrossed in work-related diversions that gradually devolve into something far less productive. If you've ever gotten lost in a Wikipedia rabbit hole, you'll understand what I'm talking about. This is only one example of unnecessary bustle that will prevent you from achieving your objectives. So, what can you do to stay on track and prevent procrastinating? If you truly want to overcome procrastination, you will need to do the following:

- Figure out how to divide each activity into smaller portions. People frequently postpone because they are overwhelmed and don't know where to begin, so they just don't begin at all.

However, breaking things down will allow you to work through each phase at a more reasonable pace.

- Remove as many distractions as possible. For example, if you want to produce one blog post every week but are always being sidetracked by other things online, consider writing the initial draft by hand or turning off your internet while you write. Remove any friction that is impeding your development and you will find it much simpler to achieve actual progress.

- Ensure that you have the necessary tools to do the work at hand. For example, if you're a social media manager attempting to handle 8 customers and 24 different social media profiles without the necessary tools, you're going to struggle. Using a social media management tool like Agorapulse to streamline your social media management will drastically lower your stress (and make procrastination a thing of the past!)

Remember that any progress you make toward your objectives, no matter how tiny, is progress. Be kind with yourself, and keep in mind that Rome was not built in a day!

4. A lack of assistance

Trying to pursue our goals in isolation might be difficult. Surrounding yourself with a supportive network of friends, family, mentors, or like-minded people may give the motivation and accountability you need to stay motivated. Seek out people who have similar goals to yours or who have already achieved them. Their expertise, counsel, and shared experiences can assist you in navigating hurdles and remaining focused on your quest.

5. Self-defeating thoughts

Negative self-talk occurs when your inner voice is overly critical, sounding more like an inner critic attempting to ruin your happiness. It's the voice in your brain telling you, "You're terrible at writing; you'll never get a job." (OK, maybe that's how my nasty self-talk sounds, but you get the point). That type of criticism will erode your confidence and make you feel like a complete failure before you ever begin. Not surprisingly, this way of thinking has a significant influence on our capacity to achieve our goals, and has even been connected to greater levels of stress and an increased risk of mental health problems. So, what are your alternatives? Replace self-limiting thoughts with affirmations that strengthen your strengths and success potential. Remember to take care of yourself and appreciate even the little victories to keep yourself motivated. Get rid of anyone who is a source of poisonous and damaging negativity in your life. You don't need folks who are simply going to pull you down and waste your time and energy.

It is possible to achieve your objectives. Goal achievement involves both effort and self-awareness. Recognizing and tackling the five typical issues described in this chapter —fear of failure, lack of clarity, procrastination, lack of support, and negative—can help you overcome these difficulties.

Remember that success is not always a straight line, and that setbacks are an unavoidable part of the path. Accept the difficulties, learn from them, and keep going ahead. You can overcome these hurdles and achieve your goals if you have endurance, drive, and a supportive mentality.

Overcoming Challenges in Goal Attainment

Setting objectives is an important part of personal and professional growth since it provides individuals and organizations with a road map to success. However, the route to goal achievement is rarely easy. Challenges, challenges, and unexpected setbacks frequently arise, requiring individuals and leaders to successfully manage and overcome them. In this examination, we will look at the numerous obstacles to goal achievement and examine techniques for overcoming them.

1. Unclear or Unrealistic Objectives

Setting targets that are either too unclear or excessively ambitious is one of the most difficult obstacles in goal achievement. Uncertain goals confuse team members, resulting in a lack of direction and motivation. Unrealistic ambitions, on the other hand, can demoralize people when they discover they are out of reach.

Strategy: Begin by identifying and refining your objectives. Make sure they are SMART (specific, measurable, attainable, relevant, and time-bound). Involve stakeholders in the goal-setting process to collect varied viewpoints and ideas, developing a shared understanding and commitment to the goals.

2. Insufficient Planning and Resources

Even the most well-defined goals might remain illusive without a sound strategy and the required resources. Inadequate planning can lead to inefficient procedures, wasteful resource allocation, and an overall lack of readiness for possible issues.

Strategy: Invest time in thorough planning. Divide the aim into smaller, more doable tasks, and spend resources wisely. Conduct a complete assessment of the necessary resources, including persons, funds, and technology. Review and revise the plan on a regular basis to adjust to changing conditions.

3. Change Resistance

Goal achievement requires change, and resistance to change is a typical problem that can stymie progress. People may be content with the status quo and avoid embracing new approaches or unfamiliar procedures.

Strategy: Promote an open and communicative culture. Communicate the goals' motivations and the rewards that will accrue from meeting them. Allow team members to raise concerns and give suggestions during the decision-making process. Provide assistance and training to make the move easier.

4. Absence of Motivation

Maintaining motivation over time may be difficult, especially when faced with setbacks or slow progress. Individuals and teams may become burned out, resulting in a loss of passion and dedication to the objective.

Strategy: Create a motivating environment by recognizing and applauding minor successes. Divide the objective into smaller milestones and recognize accomplishments along the way. Encourage cooperation and teamwork, as well as a feeling of common purpose and accountability. To enhance morale, provide constant feedback and acknowledgment.

5. Unforeseen Events and External Factors**

External circumstances like economic downturns, global crises, or industry changes can all have a substantial influence on target achievement. Unexpected occurrences, such as natural catastrophes or abrupt market movements, may interrupt planning and need a rethink of objectives. Build flexibility into your goal-setting approach. Prepare for probable external issues by developing contingency plans. Assess the external environment on a regular basis and alter goals and methods as needed. Individuals and teams must be adaptable and resilient, according to the research.

6. Ineffective Communication

Goal achievement requires effective communication. Miscommunication or a lack of communication can result in misunderstandings, competing priorities, and collaborative breakdown.

Strategy: Establish clear communication routes and procedures as a strategy. Update all stakeholders on the goals' progress, problems, and adjustments on a regular basis. Encourage open and honest communication, and resolve disagreements as soon as possible. Make use of technology and techniques to improve communication efficiency.

7. Absence of Accountability

Individuals and teams that are not held accountable for their responsibilities in achieving goals may experience a diffusion of accountability and a lack of ownership. This lack of responsibility can lead to missed deadlines, unfinished work, and mission failure overall.

Strategy: From the start, establish clear lines of accountability. Define each team member's tasks and responsibilities, and ensure that everyone knows their contribution to the larger objective. Implement frequent check-ins and performance evaluations to track progress and resolve any concerns as they arise.

8. Inadequate Adaptability

Goals may become obsolete or require revision as a result of changing circumstances, new possibilities, or new information. Failure to adapt and adjust goals as needed might result in the pursuit of outmoded or ineffective goals.

Strategy: Adopt a philosophy of constant improvement. Assess the relevance of goals on a regular basis in light of changing conditions. Encourage a learning and adaption culture in which changes are viewed as chances for progress rather than failures.

Overcoming obstacles to goal achievement is a continuous process that involves tenacity, adaptation, and good leadership. Individuals and organizations can navigate the complexities of goal-setting and increase their chances of success by addressing issues such as unclear goals, inadequate planning, resistance to change, lack of motivation, external factors, poor communication, lack of accountability, and insufficient adaptability. Adopting a proactive and strategic approach to solving problems allows people and teams to not only achieve their goals, but also thrive in a constantly changing environment.

Tracking Progress and Adjusting Strategies

The capacity to assess progress and change plans is critical for long-term success in the changing terrain of leadership. Leaders that take a proactive and flexible approach to achieving their objectives are better positioned to negotiate problems, capitalize on opportunities, and lead their teams to continual development. This chapter delves into the complexities of measuring success and changing plans, emphasizing their importance in the context of responsible leadership.

Understanding the Importance of Progress Monitoring

Accountable leaders understand that accomplishing long-term objectives takes more than just setting goals; it necessitates a methodical strategy to tracking progress. Progress tracking serves numerous important purposes:

1. Performance Evaluation:

Regularly analyzing progress enables leaders to objectively analyze individual and team performance. This evaluation indicates areas of strength and areas that may require development.

2. Resource Allocation:

Monitoring progress allows leaders to properly deploy resources. Leaders may make educated judgments about where to devote time, labor, and financial resources by recognizing which methods are producing positive results and which are not.

3. Team Morale and drive:

Celebrating milestones and recognizing successes along the road enhances team morale and drive. Recognizing progress helps to maintain a healthy culture by instilling a sense of accomplishment in team members.

Implementing Efficient Progress Monitoring Mechanisms

1. Defining Clear measurements:

Leaders must develop clear and quantifiable measurements that are consistent with their aims. Having defined metrics, whether for sales objectives, project timetables, or team performance indicators, gives a real framework for measuring success.

2. Regular Check-Ins and Reporting:

Regular check-ins and progress reports are required to keep everyone on the same page. This encourages open communication, transparency, and helps leaders to spot possible problems early on.

3. Using Technology:

In this day and age, leaders have access to a variety of tools and software that aid in progress tracking. For executives looking for real-time insights into their team's performance, project management tools, data analytics, and key performance indicator (KPI) dashboards are essential resources.

Strategy Adjustment

Tracking progress is not a one-time event; it is the first step toward informed decision-making and strategic changes. Leaders must be excellent at identifying when a change in approach is required and be adaptable. Here's why modifying strategy is such an important part of accountable leadership:

1. Market Dynamics and Outside Influences:
External influences like as market trends, technical breakthroughs, and economic upheavals can all have an impact on the efficacy of well-planned initiatives. Leaders must be aware of these developments and be willing to adapt their strategies accordingly.

2. Feedback and Learnings:
Gathering input from team members, clients, and stakeholders on a regular basis delivers useful insights. Actively seeking and analyzing feedback allows leaders to discover areas for growth and alter strategy based on lessons gained.

3. Risk Management:
The corporate environment is fundamentally dangerous. When unforeseen obstacles develop, leaders must be ready to alter their tactics. Whether it's a rapid market change, a technology upheaval, or unexpected challenges, the capacity to pivot is critical for risk mitigation.

Adjustment Success Strategies

1. Decision-Making Based on Data:
Leaders should base their decisions on facts and analytics. Data-driven insights give an impartial foundation for identifying which methods are effective and where changes are required.

2. Efficient Communication:
Communication is critical while altering strategy. Leaders must clearly describe the reasons for the change, the anticipated outcomes, and each team member's involvement in adopting the new strategy. Transparent communication fosters confidence and ensures that the team responds as a whole.

3. Agile Leadership:
The principle of agility is critical when it comes to modifying strategy. Agile leaders accept change, inspire innovation, and build an adaptable culture. Leaders with this approach may handle uncertainty

with resilience and confidence.

Case Studies of Progress Tracking and Strategy Adjustment
Apple Inc.

Apple's success may be ascribed not just to its original products, but also to its ability to modify methods in response to market input. The organization monitors product performance, customer satisfaction, and market developments on a constant basis, resulting in rapid changes to design, features, and marketing tactics.

NASA's Mars Rover Missions

NASA's Mars rover missions demonstrate the value of real-time progress tracking. The space agency checks the rover's performance on each trip and modifies its path, experiments, and communication procedures based on the data obtained. This versatility has aided the success of several rover expeditions.

Progress Tracking and Strategy Adjustment Challenges

While measuring progress and changing plans are essential components of accountable leadership, various obstacles might obstruct these processes:

1. Resistance to Change:

Team members may be resistant to changes to established practices, necessitating leaders to address concerns and clearly articulate the benefits of changes.

2. Inadequate Data:

Leaders may lack adequate facts in some circumstances to make educated judgments. This emphasizes the need of gathering relevant data and putting in place efficient tracking measures.

3. Excessive Adjustment:

A precise balance must be struck between essential changes and over adjustment. Leaders must avoid making rash decisions and verify that changes are consistent with the overall aims.

Accountable leadership is dependent on the capacity to painstakingly track progress and successfully alter tactics. Leaders that emphasize these behaviors promote a culture of continuous improvement, enabling their teams to adapt to changing problems and capitalize on new possibilities. Leaders may guide their firms toward long-term success in today's dynamic and competitive market by grasping the value of progress tracking, establishing robust processes, and embracing the art of strategic adjustment.

TRANSPARENCY IN LEADERSHIP

Transparency is a critical characteristic that may significantly improve the efficacy of leadership in any business. Transparency allows leaders to develop trust, improve communication, inspire collaboration, and overcome obstacles. The importance of openness in leadership, its impact on team dynamics, and ways for adopting and monitoring its efficacy will be discussed in this chapter.

Understanding Leadership Transparency

In a leadership environment, transparency refers to the open sharing of information, decision-making processes, and accountability. It is about being truthful, direct, and unambiguous in all facets of leadership. Transparency fosters team trust, encourages open communication, and allows for successful cooperation. Transparency is not only communicating good news or achievements, but also being open and honest about difficulties, failures, and lessons gained. It fosters an atmosphere in which everyone feels included and appreciated, promoting active involvement and input.

Transparency's Fundamental Elements

Transparency in leadership includes numerous key components that are required for its successful implementation. These components are as follows:

- Honesty: Honest communication by leaders fosters trust and confidence among team members. They are willing to providing both positive and bad facts in order to provide the workforce with a clear view of the organization's reality.

- Openness: Leaders that are open to their team members' views, ideas, and concerns foster an environment in which everyone feels appreciated and heard. They aggressively seek feedback and promote varied viewpoints, realizing that collaborative efforts frequently result in the finest solutions.

- Accountability: Leaders who accept accountability for their actions and decisions display integrity and gain their team members' respect. They hold themselves and others accountable for accomplishing objectives and exceeding expectations, building an ownership and high performance culture.
- Clarity: Leaders who deliver clear and straightforward information eliminate the possibility of uncertainty. To avoid misunderstandings, they communicate in a style that is readily understood by all team members.

Transparency's Role in Leadership

Transparency is important in leadership because it fosters trust and improves communication inside the business. Let's look at two important components of leadership transparency: developing trust and improving communication.

Transparency is the key to building trust.

Create an atmosphere of honesty, integrity, and justice. When leaders are open and honest, team members feel appreciated and respected because they know their efforts are recognized and their perspectives are heard. Reduce concerns or doubts about organizational decision-making. When leaders disclose information freely, team members receive insight into the logic behind choices, which fosters trust and understanding.

Transparency Improves Communication

Distribute pertinent information in a timely and accessible manner. Team members are more likely to feel comfortable sharing their thoughts, ideas, and concerns when leaders are honest. Encourage open and honest communication to facilitate successful problem-solving and decision-making. Leaders keep their teams informed, aligned, and engaged by delivering regular updates and feedback. Encourage a collaborative culture. Team members are more inclined to collaborate toward a single vision when leaders are open about their objectives, plans, and obstacles.

Transparency's Influence on Team Dynamics

Transparency improves team relations by fostering a collaborative atmosphere and increasing employee engagement and motivation. Let's go deeper into these two points.

Promoting a Collaborative Culture

When leaders are open and honest, team members feel more at ease discussing their ideas, issues, and points of view. This interchange of knowledge and different points of view results in better decision-making, new solutions, and overall team cohesiveness. Furthermore, openness fosters an inclusive atmosphere and psychological safety within the team. When everyone has equal access to the same information, there is no sense of exclusion or preference. As a result, all team members feel appreciated and respected, which leads to enhanced collaboration and cooperation. Finally, openness enables for the quick discovery and settlement of issues. When problems are identified, they may be handled immediately, avoiding them from escalating and negatively damaging team chemistry.

Increasing Employee Motivation and Engagement

Transparency increases employee engagement and motivation by making company objectives, expectations, and progress transparent. Employees feel more connected to the wider picture when executives communicate information about the organization's goal, strategy, and performance. Furthermore, openness stimulates employee participation in decision-making processes, providing them with a sense of ownership and empowerment. When workers understand why choices are made, they are more inclined to synchronize their efforts and actively contribute to the achievement of company goals. Transparency also enables for the acknowledgment and celebration of individual and team accomplishments. When improvements and triumphs are publicly acknowledged, morale rises and team members feel motivated to keep working at their peak.

Overcoming Obstacles to Leadership Transparency

Transparency is an essential component of good leadership because it promotes trust, collaboration, and understanding among team members. Obtaining openness, however, is not without difficulties.

Addressing Common Transparency Misconceptions

The concept that leaders must divulge every detail of decision-making processes or secret information in order to be transparent: Transparency does not imply bombarding them with irrelevant information. Instead, it is about presenting pertinent information that fosters comprehension and trust. Leaders must recognize that openness does not imply disclosing every detail of their decision-making process. It is all about providing knowledge so that team members may understand the reasoning behind choices and feel included in the process. The notion that openness results in information overload or unneeded exposure: While it is critical to be open and honest, leaders must find a balance between openness and delivering information that is useful and required for team members to efficiently carry out their jobs. Transparency should not be confused with inundating them with information. Instead, it is about providing knowledge that enables team members to make educated decisions and actively contribute to the organization's goals.

Keeping Transparency and Confidentiality in Check

While transparency is essential, leaders must also recognize the need for discretion in some instances. To safeguard individuals or the company, some information, such as personal employee data or secret business strategy, may need limited dissemination. Leaders must exercise caution when it comes to confidentiality, ensuring that it is not exploited to conceal information or create a culture of secrecy. Instead, they should talk freely about the reasons for secrecy and the restrictions that come with it. Leaders may develop trust and understanding among team members by emphasizing the value of secrecy.

Transparency in Leadership Practices Implementation

Transparency demands purposeful efforts and methods to ensure its efficacy. Let us investigate techniques for boosting openness and assessing its impact. Transparency may be increased by leaders doing the following:

- Sharing information on the organization's vision, goals, and performance on a regular basis.
- Creating open communication and feedback channels,

such as frequent team meetings or suggestion boxes.

- Promoting openness at all levels of the company and establishing a good example for others to follow.
- Giving leaders and team members training and assistance to improve their transparency abilities.

Transparency may be measured by leaders using the following criteria:

- Gathering input from team members via questionnaires, focus groups, or one-on-one conversations.
- Key performance metrics for trust, communication, cooperation, and employee satisfaction are being tracked.
- Examining decision results and the amount of comprehension among team members.

Transparency in Decision-Making

Decision-making transparency is a fundamental component of effective leadership and organizational success. Leaders are increasingly understanding the value of transparency and clarity in decision-making in today's dynamic and complicated corporate environment. This transparency not only increases confidence inside the business, but it also develops an accountability and innovation culture.

The practice of making the whole decision-making process accessible and clear to all relevant stakeholders is referred to as transparency in decision-making. It entails offering insight into the causes, considerations, and logic leading decisions, allowing everyone inside the company to understand the thinking and logic guiding such choices.

Principles of Transparent Decision-Making

1. Open Communication:

Open and honest communication is the foundation of transparent decision-making. Leaders must provide clear routes for information about choices to flow freely. Regular updates, status reports, and routes for employees to seek clarification are all part of this.

2. Information Sharing:

Transparency entails disclosing pertinent facts about the decision-making process. This includes disclosing data, research results, and any other relevant information that influenced the decision. Leaders that do so enable their people to better comprehend the context and repercussions of the decisions they make.

3. Comprehensive Decision-Making:

Decision-making is not limited to the higher echelons of leadership in a transparent environment. Leaders, on the other hand, aggressively seek opinion from a wide range of stakeholders, including workers, customers, and other relevant parties. This inclusiveness not only enhances the decision-making process, but it also fosters a sense of ownership and commitment among those who are touched by the decisions.

4. Criteria That Are Clearly Defined:

Transparent decision-making entails explicitly describing the criteria used to assess alternatives and make decisions. This ensures that all stakeholders are informed of the criteria and benchmarks that will be used to make the decision, limiting the possibility of confusion or apparent bias.

5. Consistent and Timely Communication:

Transparency necessitates rapid decision communication. Delays or discrepancies in information sharing can destroy confidence and create a sense of secrecy. Leaders must make every effort to disclose information as soon as possible, especially when actions may have a substantial impact on people or the company as a whole.

The Advantages of Decision-Making Transparency:

1. Establishing Trust:

Transparency is a vital component of organizational trust. Employees and stakeholders feel more confident when leaders are upfront about their decision-making processes, knowing that decisions are made with integrity and justice.

2. Employee Engagement:

Inclusive decision-making increases employee involvement and engagement. Individuals are more likely to be involved in the success of a company when they believe their ideas are appreciated and considered.

3. Better Problem-Solving Skills:

Transparency promotes a more collaborative approach to issue resolution. Organizations may draw into a variety of various ideas and experiences by openly addressing difficulties and including relevant stakeholders in decision-making.

4. Better adaptation:

Transparent decision-making promotes adaptation. Individuals are more willing to embrace change and collaborate toward common goals when they grasp the logic behind decisions.

5. Lower Change Resistance:

Transparent communication reduces resistance to change. Employees are more likely to embrace and support organizational changes when leaders openly communicate the rationale for a decision and the anticipated advantages.

6. Organizational Learning:

Transparency fosters a culture of lifelong learning. When choices are made publicly, both triumphs and mistakes become tremendous learning opportunities for the whole business.

Difficulties and Considerations:

While transparency in decision-making has various advantages, there are certain drawbacks to consider:

1. Maintaining Transparency while Maintaining Confidentiality:

Leaders must establish a balance between openness and secrecy, particularly in delicate situations. Certain information may be required to be kept private for legal or strategic reasons.

2. Excessive communication:

There is a risk of overcommunication, in which leaders overwhelm stakeholders with irrelevant facts. It is critical to provide the appropriate quantity of information in order to preserve clarity while not overloading recipients.

3. Vulnerability:

Leaders who are transparent must be prepared to be vulnerable and recognize when they do not have all of the answers. This transparency may promote trust, but leaders must be comfortable with the inherent uncertainty that comes with it.

Transparency in decision-making is more than a cliché; it is a necessary component of good leadership. It serves as the foundation for encouraging cooperation and achieving corporate success. Transparency will be a crucial difference in developing resilient and healthy businesses as executives continue to negotiate the challenges of the current business world. Leaders may create a culture of openness that pervades every level of the business by encouraging open communication, inclusive decision-making, and a commitment to sharing information. Finally, the benefits of open decision-making extend beyond the immediate decisions made; they contribute to the organization's general health and viability in the long run.

Balancing Transparency and Confidentiality

Transparency is critical for establishing confidence in a company and sustaining a productive work environment. Transparency, according to Forbes, is "the process of being open, honest, and straightforward about various company operations." When done correctly, the process is intended to provide workers with the knowledge they require to boost motivation and productivity in their roles and contribute to the overall success of the firm. To reap the same advantages in your organization, you must be transparent with all stakeholders while maintaining the required discretion to keep corporate objectives and long-term strategies on track.

How Transparency Can Help Your Business

As organizational transparency has gained prominence, many business owners have decided to plunge in headfirst and commit to implementing it in their organization, where they are now experiencing the benefits. Bridgewater Associates founder Ray Dalio is an outstanding example. He claims that radical transparency aided him in building his firm into the world's largest hedge fund. Transparency, according to Ray, works because it "allows everyone to express their thoughts about what's going on, which improves two-way communication, yields better ideas, and ties employees to the company's mission." Consumers care about the openness of the firms they buy from, according to studies, with 94% of respondents indicating they'd be loyal consumers if the company gave greater transparency. Everyone benefits from a transparent work environment: Employees provide leaders with crucial trust and open communication. That means they can make educated decisions about the company's future and be certain that their staff will be ready and prepared to carry them out. HR representatives are well-versed with the goals, values, and inadequacies of each team. That means businesses may hire talented people to cover critical gaps and improve team dynamics.

Managers form strong bonds with their direct subordinates by providing and receiving honest feedback. That means businesses can handle issues faster, and their team members can grow and learn more quickly. Employees converse more effectively with one another. That implies they can solve problems faster and come up with new ideas to propel the firm ahead. Customers and investors benefit from improved service and knowledge. Employees are more willing to acknowledge faults like lost orders or missing quarterly targets when they feel encouraged and valued. However, transparency does not occur by itself; it must be initiated from the top.

What Happens When Transparency Is Misaligned?

When transparency is not a company standard, the organization becomes dysfunctional. Employees soon disconnect, and productivity plummets. Either that, or they suffer from animosity and can occasionally create a toxic work atmosphere. When leaders lack openness, they lose touch with their staff and fail to relate the purpose to their daily operations. This gap generates an unproductive environment in which "busy work" is completed but no real outcomes are produced. However, too much transparency might be problematic.

Transparency, for example, becomes a problem when confidential one-on-one information is shared or televised. Similarly, releasing information regarding major changes like as mergers can leave employees with more questions than answers and a lot of concern. If the necessary foundation of trust and respect has not been established, the "tell it like it is" mindset can leave employees afraid and concerned about having their failings exposed. It can also lead to employees revolting against accountability and developing a dishonest culture (blame game, system cheating, and so on). Whatever your intentions, without trust, secrecy seems to be secret-keeping, and transparency is considered to be dishonest. As a business owner, you must strike a balance between transparency and secrecy. The only way to accomplish so is to first set a good example and build trust. It's All About Trust When It Comes to Balancing Transparency and

Confidentiality in Your Business

Only by starting with trust can you build a positive inverse connection between transparency and secrecy. After all, the purpose of openness should be ethical, not imposed to achieve desired employee behavior. Here's how you create a healthy culture of transparency while maintaining anonymity.

1: Concentrate on Your Core Values

Setting and sticking to expectations is essential for developing trust. Your company's basic values provide an excellent framework of transparency expectations and practices. Employees will know what to anticipate from the start if you tie your daily actions to your fundamental principles. They will also understand when plans must alter.

2: Keep Major Decisions Separate Until You Have a Coordinated Action Plan

If you have huge plans in the works, such as a merger, acquisition, or extensive corporate reorganization, it's essential to have a clear plan of action and iron out all the wrinkles before making that information public. Employees will understandably be anxious when things change. So, in order to maintain confidence, you must have a clear, united action plan. So, arrange things privately first, then discuss them with staff when the time comes. Because you can specify which team members may see what information, the Align program can assist you in maintaining communication secrecy.

3: Demonstrate your trustworthiness by delegating tasks.

If you can't let go and delegate work to your staff, they'll never feel genuinely trusted. So, show your staff that you trust them to make excellent judgments by allowing them to do so. Our software makes it simple to assign assignments to members of your team. You might also feel at ease giving over the reins by aligning crucial metrics to their new duties.

4: Encourage Transparency and Anonymity Feedback

Because trust is founded on mutual understanding, it is critical to maintain an open channel of communication for workers and members to offer feedback. eNPS surveys are a quick, effective, and consistent approach to measure the sentiment of your employees, allowing you to respond immediately to concerns or do more of what is currently working. These surveys are a huge step toward building trust since they are anonymous, allowing employees to provide honest feedback without fear of punishment.

5 Communicate frequently and effectively.

We cannot emphasize this enough. Clear communication is the cornerstone of trust; therefore, you should communicate with your staff on a regular basis—in good and bad times. Using eNPS surveys to solicit anonymous feedback is an important first step. Taking the extra step to request feedback in person, on the other hand, may help you create trust and improve the relationship between managers and direct reports. In-person conversation also provides context that surveys cannot always provide. Align facilitates communication with your teams by providing metrics-driven performance management. Our format allows you to swiftly examine day-to-day actions and KPIs, allowing you more time to dig deeper. Align Can Help You Improve Your Company Culture. The more employees are aware of and feel engaged in corporate operations, the more likely they are to provide the honest, critical feedback required to overcome barriers and solve issues. And when everyone feels trusted and encouraged, they are more likely to love their work and work more. It's time to put openness and secrecy to work in your business so you can spend less time dealing with problems and more time achieving your objectives.

EMBRACING RESPONSIBILITY IN LEADERSHIP

Accepting accountability is essential for good leadership. Leaders who understand the value of taking responsibility and being accountable for their actions create an environment favorable to success in a quickly growing and complicated world. This essay digs into the numerous dimensions of leadership responsibility, analyzing its relevance, problems, and tactics for establishing an accountability culture.

Understanding Leadership Responsibility

Leadership responsibility extends beyond just carrying out duties or making choices. It entails a greater dedication to the results of those decisions and activities. Leaders who accept responsibility understand the influence of their decisions on the business, its people, and the larger community. This sense of accountability serves as the foundation for trust and credibility, both of which are required for effective leadership.

The Relationship Between Responsibility and Trust

In leadership, trust is a delicate but vital commodity. Accepting responsibility is strongly related to developing and keeping trust. When leaders accept responsibility for their actions, whether positive or bad, it sends a strong message to their team that they can be counted on to act in the best interests of the business. A team's glue is trust, and good leadership is the catalyst for its establishment.

Responsibility vs. accountability

What distinguishes a good leader from a terrible one? Some may say that excellent leadership is all about vision, smart decision-making, and inspiring people to do their best. All of these are characteristics that we normally connect with outstanding leaders. But what role do accountability and responsibility have in a leader's capacity to lead effectively? And, when it comes to leadership, which is more important: responsibility or accountability?

In this essay, we will define these two concepts and compare and contrast accountability and responsibility. We'll also give you some pointers on how to develop your skills in these areas and correctly emphasize them on your CV.

What's the difference between responsibility and accountability?

When things go wrong at work, people frequently reply with tired excuses like "it's not my job" or "it's not my fault!" These typical refrains are employed in order to evade both blame and accountability. Worse, the two terms are frequently used interchangeably, as if they signify the same thing. In truth, the two terms symbolize completely distinct notions, despite the fact that both are critical for effective leadership. To further grasp what each of these phrases entails, let's look at them independently and then compare them.

What exactly is responsibility?

The idea of responsibility focuses on tasks and responsibilities. Responsibilities are delegated with the assumption that you will accomplish specific outcomes. For example, you may be in charge of completing certain activities that are necessary to accomplish a particular result. Responsibility for the outcome may even be delegated to numerous persons, each of whom undertakes specialized activities in pursuit of a shared objective. To be responsible, you must be able to complete whatever jobs and objectives are assigned to you. Obviously, no one would assign a task that was well above the capability of a freshly hired and utterly untrained employee. After all, blaming that individual if the assignment was not completed adequately would be absurd.

What exactly is accountability?

Accountability includes responsibility, but it extends much beyond being accountable for certain tasks and obligations. True accountability is not just accepting and owning blame, but also being held accountable for the consequences of your actions. Furthermore, your accountability is to other people, not the task: your team, subordinates, superiors, shareholders, clients, and so on. Being responsible may sound like you just get blame when something goes wrong, but it may also mean you earn credit when things go well. True responsibility simply means that you are willing to answer for the consequences of your decisions and actions, whether at work or in your personal life. When your decisions or activities result in beneficial outcomes, you should be prepared to accept your fair part of the credit. Alternatively, you must be willing to accept responsibility for poor judgments and behaviors that result in unfavorable results. Former President Harry S. Truman, for example, famously had a sign on his desk that said, "The Buck Stops Here." Truman mentioned the sign in his farewell address to the country, saying, "The President - whoever he is - has to decide." He can't blame it on anyone. Nobody else can make the decision for him. That is his responsibility." Truman realized that, as President, he was not only responsible for decision-making, but also for everything that happened during his presidency.

The distinctions between responsible and accountable

So, what exactly are the distinctions between accountability and responsibility? What comes to mind when you think of the difference between responsibility and accountability? Below, we'll look at several critical elements that can help you distinguish between these two concepts. Accountability must be acknowledged before responsibility can be assigned. Accountability tends to rest on one person's shoulders; responsibility might be shared by numerous persons. It is possible to be accountable for something without being accountable for the outcome. In other words, people are responsible for obligations and tasks while they are being accomplished, but genuine responsibility occurs after the fact. Frequently, the person ultimately responsible for an outcome is the same person who delegated responsibility for that outcome to others.

Responsibility, as you can see, is a more flexible idea that might entail a single individual with given responsibilities or a group of people who are all equally accountable for getting things done. However, in nearly every case, accountability falls on a single person: the leader. That is why exceptional leaders are distinguished by more than simply their obligations, which solely represent their assigned jobs and tasks. They are also defined by their willingness to accept responsibility for the results of their decisions and actions. It's also worth noting that responsibility is a fundamental component of any strong corporate culture. If your workplace fosters a sense of accountability, it is likely to have greater levels of employee engagement, overall productivity, and a shared team vision. Leaders in companies with this sort of accountability-focused culture are held accountable to people around them.

Tips for becoming more accountable

Of course, it's one thing to recognize the critical role that accountability can play in any company's leadership. The true issue most aspiring leaders should be asking is how to build the character attributes required to be a more accountable leader or manager. Fortunately, this is not some enigmatic feature that only a select few may acquire. Instead, anybody may cultivate a sense of accountability in both their personal and professional life. Equally important, excellent leaders can instill a higher feeling of accountability in their employees by incorporating it into their leadership style and corporate culture. To get started, you must first focus on enhancing your personal and professional accountability. The following suggestions may be useful.

Make your promise your bond.

When you accept to be held accountable for anything, you are basically saying that you will do everything possible to achieve the intended objectives. To keep that pledge, you must be able to hold yourself accountable by making a practice of keeping your promises.

Establish clear expectations.

Make sure that people understand what you anticipate from them as you build your own accountability attributes. Set specific goals and describe how success will be judged. You should also aim to clarify your personal leadership expectations and how they might assist you be accountable for the team's results.

Set a good example

Effective leadership necessitates personal accountability, but it also necessitates a culture that values accountability. You should set an example for everyone in your company by demonstrating that you hold yourself and your team accountable for your failures and triumphs. That example can motivate others to take responsibility of their work, resulting in increased motivation and productivity, raising the performance and accountability standard for everyone in the organization.

Give your team members authority.

One important part of responsibility that many leaders overlook is the empowering of people around them. It is simpler to generate the outcomes you require when you assist others in being their best. Because there would be less possibility of bad results, you will find it simpler to develop the practice of accepting accountability.

Allow the buck to stop at your desk.

It might be tempting to blame others for your failings rather than examine your own. If you want to become a more accountable person and leader, you should always start by looking in the mirror. What might you have done differently to get a better result? Did you pass up possibilities to assist your team in achieving greater results?

You may also be wondering what this implication for your CV. How can you demonstrate your accountability to prospective employers? It's not as difficult as you may think. The idea is to concentrate on what you've been held accountable for rather than just stating your obligations and responsibilities. Don't just write, "responsible for managing team training." Instead, draw attention to accountability by emphasizing what you accomplished: "Managed continuing sales team training for 60 employees, boosting team engagement, improving retention by 42%, and increasing sales revenue by 22% in one quarter."

Making your obligations and responsibilities into quantifiable achievements will demonstrate your accountability to hiring supervisors. When you do this for each of the bullet point examples you offer with your job ads, you can transform your resume's professional experience section into a showcase of responsibility. Learn the difference between responsibility and accountability to become a more successful leader! The distinction between duty and accountability may appear perplexing at first, but it's pretty simple after you study each notion. Of course, everyone has obligations, but genuine leaders assume responsibility for how those tasks are handled. Understanding this basic concept will help you become the sort of leader who can always achieve his or her professional and personal goals!

Taking Ownership of Mistakes

In the area of leadership, the ability to accept responsibility for mistakes is a sign of true accountability. It is a trait that not only identifies a leader's character but also affects the culture of a company. Leaders who accept and demonstrate accountability in the face of mistakes establish a climate that promotes learning, development, and continual progress. For various reasons, accepting responsibility for mistakes is an essential component of accountable leadership. For starters, it exhibits humility. Leaders who freely admit their mistakes convey a strong message to their teams: no one is perfect, and mistakes are part of the process. This humility fosters trust and creates a more genuine bond between leaders and their teams. Second, accepting ownership promotes a culture of accountability. When leaders take responsibility for their actions, it establishes a precedent for everyone else in the organization. When team members witness their leaders taking responsibility for their own mistakes, they are more inclined to do the same. This sense of shared responsibility helps to a more healthy and resilient company culture.

The Learning Possibility

Mistakes are unavoidable, but what distinguishes accountable leaders is their ability to transform these errors into great learning opportunities. Rather from seeing mistakes as setbacks, these leaders embrace them as opportunities for growth. When a leader accepts responsibility for a mistake, they create an environment in which learning takes precedence over blaming. Leaders may evaluate the core reasons of the error, identify areas for improvement, and execute changes to prevent such failures in the future by accepting ownership. This proactive attitude to learning from failures benefits not just the leader, but also the overall performance and effectiveness of the team.

Overcoming Consequences Fear

The fear of consequences is one reason leaders may be hesitant to accept responsibility for mistakes. Admitting mistake may be viewed as a sign of weakness or ineptitude in some work cultures. responsible leaders, on the other hand, understand that the short-term unpleasantness of acknowledging a mistake is significantly exceeded by the long-term rewards of open and responsible leadership. Leaders may reduce the fear of acknowledging mistakes by fostering a climate in which taking ownership is encouraged and supported. As a result, team members are more candid about their own mistakes, establishing a culture of honesty and continual growth.

Trust-Building Through Vulnerability

Any effective leader-team connection is built on trust. When leaders accept responsibility for their mistakes, they demonstrate vulnerability – a strong trait that fosters team trust. Team members are more inclined to trust a leader who is willing to acknowledge when they are incorrect because it humanizes and relatable the boss. Furthermore, this vulnerability prepares the groundwork for open communication. When leaders demonstrate taking responsibility, they foster a culture in which team members feel comfortable voicing their concerns, making changes, and openly addressing issues. This open channel of communication fosters cooperation and creativity throughout the business.

Using a Systematic Approach

Taking responsibility for mistakes entails more than just verbalizing responsibilities; it also entails executing a systematic method to addressing and correcting errors. Accountable leaders create methods to objectively assess mistakes, concentrating on understanding the underlying reasons rather than assigning blame. This methodical technique frequently includes doing post-mortem studies, developing feedback loops, and putting remedial measures in place. Leaders establish a foundation for continuous improvement that pervades the organization by implementing these approaches.

Effective Ownership Communication

When it comes to accepting responsibility for mistakes, communication is essential. Leaders must express their regret for the error in a straightforward and honest manner. This includes publicly acknowledging the consequences of the error, laying out the efforts being taken to correct the problem, and explaining the lessons learned.

Effective communication in the face of errors not only indicates accountability, but also reassures the team that the leader is actively involved in fixing the issue. It limits the spread of disinformation and rumors, preserving the organization's feeling of trust and stability.

Setting a good example

Taking responsibility for mistakes is not a one-time occurrence, but rather a continuous commitment to accountability. Leaders must continuously model this conduct, proving to their teams that accountability is not a desirable characteristic, but rather a basic component of their leadership philosophy. Accountable leaders motivate their people to adopt a similar mentality by setting a good example. When team members see their leaders constantly accepting responsibility for mistakes and learning from them, a ripple effect occurs, producing a culture in which accountability is firmly established in the corporate DNA.

Taking responsibility for mistakes emerges as a core part of accountable leadership in the complicated terrain of leadership. It entails more than just acknowledgment; it entails a commitment to learning, a commitment to ongoing growth, and the bravery to embrace vulnerability. Leaders that emphasize accountability in the face of mistakes foster a culture of trust, responsibility, and resilience among their businesses. They not only improve their individual leadership effectiveness, but they also add to the whole team's long-term success and sustainability.

Taking Ownership of Mistakes as a Mark of Leadership

What makes you a trustworthy leader is not whether or not you make any mistakes. You will undoubtedly make some mistakes since true leadership involves dealing with uncertain outcomes. It's about whether you're capable of admitting your errors and dealing with them with honesty, integrity, and grace. When the finest leaders make a mistake, it does not make them less trustworthy. They gain trust exactly because of how they own and control the process.

The Value of Admitting When You're Wrong

Previously, research conducted across 3,100 workers in 13 countries indicated that the most significant difference in leadership behavior between what important to employees and what is seen to be routinely displayed by supervisors is: "admitting when they are wrong." Eighty-one percent of employees said it was critical or very important for leaders to confess mistakes, but just 41 percent thought their managers did so on a regular basis. According to the researchers, a leader's readiness to "admit when they are wrong" is the most tested conduct when it comes to positively impacting employee job satisfaction and desire to continue on the work.

The Risk of Deflection or Deniability

An unwillingness to see and confess mistakes is a weakness, not a strength - and it is blinding and hazardous in a leader. Nobody loves being wrong, and Psychology Today reminds out that we sometimes accept complete responsibility for mistakes and sometimes just partial blame, but this is not the same as a predisposition to "push back against the actual facts." Psychological rigidity occurs when a person repeatedly rejects all facts and is just unable to accept, he or she is incorrect. "Some people have such a fragile ego, such brittle self-esteem, such a weak "psychological constitution," that admitting they made a mistake or that they were wrong is fundamentally too threatening for their egos to tolerate," says Guy Winch, Ph.D., in his book "The Ego's Guide to Self-Esteem." "Because admitting they were wrong and absorbing that reality would be so psychologically damaging, their defense mechanisms do something remarkable to avoid doing so — they literally distort their perception of reality to make it (reality) less threatening." Their defensive systems safeguard their fragile ego by altering the facts in their minds, making them no longer wrong or accountable."

Winch adds out that this individual may appear to be maintaining their ground and not backing down, and we could link this conduct with being powerful, yet it is everything but. "These people are not choosing to stand their ground; they're compelled to do so in order to protect their fragile egos..." said Winch. "It takes a certain amount of emotional strength and courage to deal with that reality and own up to our mistakes." If someone is unable to accept a mistake in the face of obvious proof, if they must blame someone else, deflect, or change the story, it is because their ego is too fragile to allow the humility (or humanity) of erring. That is the inverse of leadership. On a lighter note, not openly recognizing a mistake or glossing over it might indicate a lack of knowledge in the benefits of doing so for progress. "Any great leader will tell you that they have made a lot of mistakes along the way." "They will admit that collective insight from bad decisions taught them invaluable lessons - and how to see opportunities in everything and anticipate the unexpected more quickly," says Forbes author Glenn Lopis. "Successful leaders are honest enough with themselves and others to admit their mistakes so that those around them can benefit from their experiences." Many leaders lack this understanding because they are too arrogant to accept mistakes as great learning opportunities for themselves and others."

Owning Mistakes Alchemy = Trust

"Being a leader doesn't mean that you're always right or that you won't err," says Jim Whitehurst, the president and CEO of Red Hat. "What being a leader does mean is airing the reasons for why you did something and then making yourself accountable for the results—even if those you're accountable to don't directly work for you." Admitting and accepting responsibility for a mistake implies a desire to demonstrate human frailty and transparency, which fosters trust, increases your credibility as a leader, and gets respect. "When leaders realize they've made a mistake, others usually notice as well." bosses who refuse to confess they were wrong give employees with the impression that their bosses value being right over being honest," argues Chris McCloskey of Dale Carnegie Training. "Taking responsibility demonstrates that leaders value integrity over the easier paths of blaming others or hoping their error goes unnoticed." Admitting when you're wrong also demonstrates that you're aware of, and thus able to learn from, your mistakes. This might increase your confidence in your leadership."

As a leader, owning your mistake offers a vital sense of safety and adds credibility to your words. When workers feel comfortable, they devote their skills and resources to supporting the leader rather than defending their place in the business, while also fostering a culture in which employees may feel safe to take significant risks and own their errors. Reina Trust Building consultants' Michelle Reina states, "Through nearly 25 years of trust-focused research and experience, we can give one piece of guidance to leaders seeking to increase their trustworthiness: Take responsibility for your mistakes." She says, "Do you remember the last time you didn't just 'get through' a mistake, but embraced it as a ready-made opportunity to deepen trust?" According to Reina, the honesty, integrity, and safety gained by acknowledging a mistake and then addressing problems catalyzes trust: "In our experience, when you admit you've made a mistake, you don't erode trust in your leadership, you strengthen it."

What Women Should Keep in Mind

According to research, women are more prone to emotionally hang on to mistakes and blame themselves, whereas males move on faster, construct "tidy stories" about mistakes, or have detached opinions on them. So, although recognizing true errors is vital, it's also crucial for women to realize that owning a mistake does not excuse or demand self-shaming. And this isn't about apologizing all the time, which is certainly something to avoid. Owning a true mistake is acknowledging and learning from an obviously faulty judgment or decision as something you are capable of as a person. It's about knowing you're large enough to accept a mistake, not shrinking yourself. Self-shaming, on the other hand, leads to a state of "I am bad" forever making that mistake. "Women can spend less time beating themselves up and more time learning from their mistakes," argues Alina Tugenda, author of "Better by Mistake: The Unexpected Benefits of Being Wrong." "I'm not advocating blaming "the system," but being able to depersonalize the mistake helps us to view it more objectively and learn whatever lessons can be learned from it."

Managing Your Errors

Finally, making a mistake or making an incorrect judgment reflects a willingness to make decisions that involve both risk and opportunity. What important is your capacity to accept your faults without covering them up, shifting responsibility, or unnecessarily internalizing and dramatizing the mistake. Aside from acknowledging the error, leadership steps include reducing the harm, learning from your mistakes, openly working with your team to address problems, assisting others to avoid making the same mistake, and moving on. A mistake is still a mistake. The process of managing the error may serve as a springboard to more trust, respect, and appreciation for the leader. The difference, like with anything, is in how you manage it.

How to encourage your team to take responsibility

It might be tough to persuade employees that they have done something wrong. However, one of the most critical talents your team may have is the willingness to accept personal responsibility. It is your obligation as a leader to instruct them. You may inspire your team to be more accountable by sharing experiences, open communication, and leading by example.

Give Them Accountability

Giving your team responsibility is the simplest approach to persuade people to accept responsibility for themselves and their job. Teach kids how to be responsible by assigning them tasks that force them to learn. You may do this by giving them greater say and enabling them to define their own standards at work. It is critical that your staff believes in what they are doing and that you trust them. Thinking you trust them is essential for them to accept responsibility.

"When team members disagree with a leader's management style, they are less likely to accept responsibility for tasks." People are less inclined to commit if they are doing something in which they do not believe." - Astute Manager

Employees are more willing to share in the risk as well as the gain if the job you conduct with your team is viewed as a partnership, a contract of trust.

Make it Safe for People to Speak Up

Everyone makes errors, so don't pass judgment on them. If you want to inspire accountability, you must create a safe environment in which employees feel comfortable coming forward when problems develop.

"Although some leaders may fear that their employees will rock the boat by speaking up, in reality, those workers are often helping avoid a shipwreck." - Video & Strategy

While certain errors may have harsher penalties than others, make it clear to employees that acknowledging their faults will result in more respect from you and their colleagues for speaking up. Speaking out when you're incorrect might be frightening, but having the courage to do so is admirable. Remind them that accepting responsibility isn't always a bad thing. Often, discussions about personal responsibility focus solely on the negative consequences of accepting responsibility for your mistakes. However, there are several reasons why being responsibility for your actions is the better option.

Some of the benefits of accepting responsibility include:

- Higher self-esteem levels
- increased chances of future success
- It will be simpler to learn from your mistakes.
- More confidence and respect from coworkers and leaders
- Interpersonal interactions have improved.
- Increased self-assurance in future leadership roles

"A big reason why you are able to admit fault is that you recognize that once you admit what you have done wrong, you can work to make it better, and so you are not threatened by admitting mistakes." - For the Greater Good

When you remind your team of the long-term rewards of being responsible, they will be more inclined to apologize when they have made a mistake, as long as you are prepared to do the same, which brings us to the following point...

Set a good example.

Why should any of your workers feel obligated to accept responsibility for their mistakes if you would not? One of the most essential things a leader can do is set a good example, especially when it comes to accepting responsibility.

"Never ask a subordinate to perform something that you are unwilling to do... Set a positive example for others by being an effective manager and leader." - Notre Dame University

Fear of the repercussions or of being judged is at the top of the list of reasons why individuals strive to avoid responsibilities. However, errors are necessary for company success since they teach us so much. Taking responsibility forces everyone to become more aware of themselves and others. That is the most effective technique to instill trust in your staff and gain their trust. So, try these four strategies for boosting responsibility and see how they go! How do you inspire your staff to take ownership?

BUILDING TRUST

Effective leadership is built on trust. Trust is the basis upon which relationships are created, cooperation is promoted, and success is attained in any company or team. Leaders that focus and actively try to develop trust foster an environment in which people feel safe, appreciated, and driven. This in-depth investigation dives into the many facets of developing trust in leadership, evaluating the importance of trust, tactics for creating it, and the implications of its absence.

The Importance of Leadership Trust

Trust is a currency that every successful team and organization uses. Without it, communication suffers, creativity stagnates, and cooperation suffers. Trust is the glue that holds people together and allows them to work together to achieve mutual goals. Trust is vital in a leadership setting not just between leaders and their team members, but also among team members themselves. Individuals are more inclined to take chances, share ideas, and contribute fully to the communal effort when trust is present. Trust is founded on consistency, openness, and honesty. Leaders that continuously display these characteristics gain the trust of their team, resulting in a good and conducive work atmosphere. Trust is an ever-changing characteristic of leadership that needs continual work to create and sustain. It is not a one-time accomplishment, but rather a constant process that demands focus, perseverance, and genuineness.

"Trust is the life's glue." It is the most important component of good communication. It is the fundamental idea that underpins all interactions. When trust is high, communication is simple, quick, and effective. "Stephen Covey (1992) is a management consultant. Trust is a deep conviction in someone or something's dependability, veracity, or capacity. Some people are more prone to trusting people and things than others, yet trust is typically earned and difficult to regain once lost.

The Importance of trust

Effective working relationships are built on trust. The more someone trusts a colleague, manager, or team member, the more likely they will cooperate, share information, and collaborate efficiently. So trust contributes to the smooth operation of organizations by enhancing optimism, improving procedures, and driving individual and team performance. Leaders who are trusted by others are more likely to attract more and higher qualified applicants for every job opening in their teams, and they are less likely to have high staff turnover. Employees view workplaces and teams with low levels of trust as "stressful," "frustrating," "threatening," and "demotivating." According to a poll conducted by the Institute (2014), the industries and sectors with the lowest internal trust - that is, employees who did not trust their own organizations - were also not well trusted by the general public. As a result, there is a high correlation between customer and staff trust levels, as well as consumers avoiding organizations they do not trust. This is bad news for businesses in high-risk industries and sectors. According to the same study, employees in the largest organizations had the lowest levels of trust, while those in organizations with 50 or less people have the greatest levels.

Galford and Drapeau (2011) created a well-known trust formula.

$$Trustworthiness = \frac{Credibility + Reliability + Intimacy}{Self\text{-}Orientation}$$

Credibility	Words Is earned by expertise and by being up-front about your limitations
Reliability	Actions consistency and dependability
Intimacy	Emotions not about revealing personal details, but rather, making the business of the organisation personal and understanding the sensitivities of others
Self-Orientation	Motives the degree to which you focus on your own concerns when interacting with others

Developing and Earning Trust

A leader may build or strengthen trust by concentrating on six elements (Covey, 1992): The single most significant driver of trust is openness. Honesty is part of this, as is knowing that if someone makes a mistake, they will admit it. If acknowledging a mistake is tough for you, remember that no one is perfect, and covering up mistakes typically leads to bigger difficulties. Employees want clarity, to know what is expected of them by you as their leader, as well as regular feedback on their performance. Making timely judgments indicates your expertise, confidence, and competency as a leader, which reassures your staff. Integrity entails being congruent, which means that your actions do not contradict your principles. You actually "walk the walk." You do not convey one message via your words and another through your body language.

Promises and confidences must be kept with empathy and care. A reputation for commitment and dependability makes you intrinsically more trustworthy. We're primarily concerned with gaining the confidence of your staff here, but the same concepts apply to other stakeholders, including customers and suppliers. It also applies to gaining the trust of your bosses. If you believe you lack any of the trust elements described above, the workplace offers several informal learning opportunities. Simply soliciting feedback from your team, coworkers, clients, and suppliers will not only increase your self-awareness but will also help you swiftly develop key communication skills.

According to Robert Hurley (2006), a management professor at Fordham University in New York, trust is also dependent on:

- How secure the parties involved (the person who is being trusted and the person who is being trusted) feel.
- How many parallels exist between the parties?
- How well the interests of the parties are matched.
- Hurley suggests the following activities to increase security,
  similarities, and interest alignment when you are the one being trusted:

1. Spend more time outlining the alternatives and the hazards associated with each, and provide some form of safety net.
2. Use the term 'we' more frequently and the phrase 'I' less frequently. Highlight what you have in common (values, objectives, etc.).
3. Make it obvious to yourself who your interests are. Consider others' interests and try to accommodate them if feasible.

Repairing a Broken Trust

There are several ways to betray confidence. Reina & Reina (2014) provide the following examples:

- Error concealment
- Gossiping
- Keeping information hidden
- Confidential information leaking
- Micro-managing
- Assassinating the messenger
- stifling other people's thoughts
- Taking credit for the labor of others, throwing others under the bus

We may also include lying, breaking agreements and pledges arbitrarily, and any other form of cruel, inconsiderate behavior. It always takes time to rebuild trust. A psychological 'contract' has been breached and must be renegotiated. This refers to the unwritten set of job expectations as opposed to the legal employment contract. Always begin by confessing that you made a mistake or acted incorrectly. You must meet with those whose confidence has been violated and inform them of this. To demonstrate your knowledge, spell out exactly what breached the trust. Say you're sorry. Allow the injured party or parties to freely express their emotions. Actively listen to them while acknowledging their emotions. Explain what you intend to do to rebuild the shattered trust, and ensure that this is deemed appropriate. Prepare to be skeptical. Please be patient. Above all, avoid allowing your ego to get in the way. Trust may be reestablished and strengthened if skillfully repaired (Holiday, 2016).

Trust-Building Strategies for Leaders

What is the secret to improved health, greater energy, reduced stress, and enhanced productivity? The study for a piece Paul J. Zak wrote for the Harvard Business Review indicates that trust is the easy solution. Employee results increased exponentially when organizations invested time in developing trust. "74% less stress, 106% more energy at work, 50% higher productivity, 13% fewer sick days, 76% more engagement, 29% more life satisfaction, and 40% less burnout," for instance, was what respondents said. A business without faith in its leaders is akin to a ship without water. No matter how hard you try, it won't go away. Leaders start micromanaging when there is a lack of trust among team members because they believe that employees are not competent to perform their jobs. Time spent on low-priority tasks grows, which has an impact on stress levels and productivity. Executives are consequently left with less time to plan and strategize the company's future course of action. As a result, the company starts to lag behind and engage in reactive behavior. People also cease making public contributions because of fear of being rejected, judged, or ignored. Employees are unlikely to do more than the barest minimum of effort and are more likely to defect and join a rival company if there is no indication that their abilities are valued.

All organizations should prioritize developing a trusting environment. The absence of trust in the workplace hinders all the essential elements that propel a firm towards success, including creativity, innovation, teamwork, communication, productivity, and engagement. Understanding what trust is and these ten strategies for cultivating it as a leader can help you avoid creating a toxic work environment and team culture.

> Workers who feel trusted by their bosses are more productive and experience less stress.
> John Maxwell asserts that establishing trust requires consistency between words and deeds.
> Because people don't trust the leadership, seventy percent of reform initiatives fail.
> Just half of the workforce knows what the management expects of them.
> Establishing trust requires team leaders to consistently be there for their teammates.

Trust in work place: What Is It?

Believing that someone else is continuously predictable and safe is the foundation of trust, according to the American Psychological Association (APA), which defines trust as "reliance on or confidence in the dependability of someone or something." In the absence of these elements, interpersonal interactions cannot develop. It's something that gradually takes shape. Leadership guru John Maxwell says, "To be honest with you, we're withdrawing, or we're depositing into our trustworthy account," in the Minute with Maxwell video. .... How can I develop and build that reliable account? ......First of all, what I say and do are the same. .... It just goes to show that developing trust is a decision to either invest in or withdraw from other people. Secondly, I believe that reliable accounts are created when you consistently mean the best and do the best for people. Consequently, developing trust in a partnership becomes an essential ability.

The Top 10 Strategies for Developing Trust in Teams

There are many techniques that company leaders can demonstrate and impart to their team members in order to foster a trustworthy work atmosphere. Discover ten strategies for fostering trust as a manager, director, or executive below.

1. Continually fulfill your end of the bargain.

Predictability is necessary for trust. There will be little or no trust if someone believes that a leader is erratic, unstable, or untrustworthy. Maintaining consistency between your words and deeds is the best method to build trust. Don't, for instance, commit to something you can't accomplish. It may appear as though you're promising a raise in six months, but you're not sure if the company's finances can support this. Adhere to your fair expectations of yourself. Before making a choice, spend some time reverse engineering it if you're unsure. Go here to find out more about making decisions.

Proficient leaders are aware that fulfilling pledges and obligations is essential to establishing confidence. Overpromising and under delivering earns a person the reputation of being dishonest, or worse, a scammer. Disappointment and low morale prevent people from growing in respect and belief. However, trust increases in the workplace when a leader demonstrates consistency and demonstrates the worth of their words.

2. Acknowledge and correct errors as soon as you make them.

There will be moments as a leader when you make a mistake and let people down. Life involves failure. Accepting responsibility for mistakes is a crucial part of developing trust. A person in a position of authority immediately distances themselves from their reliable account when they are unable to own up to their mistakes or assign blame. This is a result of their lack of honesty and accountability in their actions. According to best-selling author and well-known speaker Simon Sinek, "competence and integrity are the two dimensions of trust." We'll overlook competent mistakes. Integrity-related errors are more difficult to correct.

Team members learn how to get back up after being knocked down by leaders who take ownership of their mistakes. They're the first in the group to own up to their errors and take the necessary steps to atone for their misdeeds. They also demonstrate to their workforce that in a forward-thinking organization, failure is expected. This kind of thinking removes perfectionism from the workplace and gives creativity and innovation a place at the table.

3. Use emotional intelligence when communicating.

Since emotional intelligence (EI) fosters deep interpersonal relationships, it is one of the most important factors in establishing trust in the workplace. Emotional intelligence is divided into four quadrants: relationship management, self-management, social awareness, and self-awareness. Establishing safe relationships with team members, clients, and consumers becomes problematic when a leader lacks proficiency in one or more of these domains. A person with low emotional intelligence, for instance, could be easily agitated, behave selfishly, or lack empathy. These characteristics all give the impression that a person is erratic and untrustworthy, which makes none of them good for building trust. The good news is that an individual's EI can rise with time.

Among the advice for raising EI is:
- identifying emotional triggers and creating a strategy to deal with them.
- establishing a routine of mindfulness.
- expressing intentions.
- Getting comments.
- Investing time in solving problems.
- Recognizing the impact of your words, deeds, and ideas on other people.
- honing your listening comprehension.
- Looking for nonverbal clues in the space.

- identifying with others instead than feeling sorry for them.
- putting aside a few hours per week to create goals and provide rewards for achieving them.
- putting in time to support your staff, mediate disputes, and promote cooperation and teamwork.

4. Handle pivots and change appropriately.

The ancient statement by philosopher Heraclitus, "The only constant in life is change," holds true for leaders who understand that innovation, adaptation, and change are key components of successful enterprises. Nevertheless, without a foundation of support and trust between managers and staff, change implementation will not be possible. Actually, according to John Kotter's seminal research published in Leading transformation, 70% of transformation initiatives were unsuccessful. The majority of this can be attributed to a lack of managerial support and employee buy-in. They must first witness the leadership effectively implementing the required changes before they can begin to learn how to trust.

Emily Lawson and Colin Price state in a McKinsey & Company paper that four factors lead to meaningful change. The first is narrating a gripping tale to highlight the implications of the change being made. Watching people in positions of leadership embody the change that is being executed is the second. The people implementing the change then need to support and reinforce it. The authors state that "behavior that people are asked to embrace must be consistent with reporting structures, management and operational processes, and measurement procedures—setting targets, measuring performance, and awarding financial and nonfinancial rewards." Lastly, leaders have to make sure that the members of their team get the direction and training they need to be able to implement the change.

5. Express your gratitude and admiration.

When leaders value and invest in their teams, trust is developed. However, studies reveal that there is a dearth of recognition at work. For instance, a Psychometrics study reveals that over 50% of workers desire greater recognition from their managers in the workplace. Team members start to disengage, disassociate, and disconnect from their leaders and the goal that the group is all working toward when they feel that they are being taken advantage of. As a leader, the greatest method to overcome this is to demonstrate to each member of the team how much they are appreciated. Team members benefit from this as they develop their ability to trust leaders.

The dynamic at work changes when leaders adopt an attitude of gratitude. "Here's a job—do it" gives way to "Thank you for what you're doing." in the tale. Your efforts are crucial to achieving our goal. We couldn't change the world without you, so please know that your gratitude and admiration are contagious. Psychologists Sara Algoe and Jonathan Haidt contend that seeing and relating to positively influencing individuals encourages others to work on themselves and build stronger bonds with others. One of the finest methods to teach leadership to your team is to model it yourself. It demonstrates to others how you live according to your principles, gradually earning their respect, influence, and trust.

6. Take judgment out of the workplace.

Judgment is the quickest method to stifle originality and inventiveness. Since judgment can be expressed both vocally and nonverbally, it can take on many different forms. It's easy for people who are targeted by it to interpret negative body language, such as rolling one's eyes and shaking one's head, or a dismissive remark. When someone feels judged, they often become insecure and reluctant to express their feelings, ideas, and views. Judgment frequently results from someone avoiding an honest discussion. Speak with the person instead than talking about them. Engage in discussion with someone before betraying their trust and making them feel insignificant, as Walt Whitman famously advised, "Be curious, not judgmental." Ask them what motivates them to believe what they do, why they think the way they do, and have an open mind as you listen. Make room for delving farther into a comprehension.

7. Never underestimate the influence of vulnerability.

Being vulnerable is essential to establishing trust. It's the glue that keeps enduring partnerships together through difficult times. This is why it is imperative that all leaders master this particular leadership ability. Brené Brown's Dare to Lead is among the best tools for learning how to lead with vulnerability. Vulnerability is "the emotion that we experience during times of uncertainty, risk, and emotional exposure," according to Brown, and it is essential to becoming a courageous, unwavering leader who builds and sustains trust.

Among the things you may practice being vulnerable are:
- having difficult talks, even when avoiding them is simple.
- having an attentive ear and approaching issues with a solution-focused approach.
- returning to the conversations that need some thought time or a new viewpoint.
- Adhering to the principles that you have chosen to guide your thoughts, words, deeds, and behaviors.
- sympathizing with someone who is facing hardship.
- presuming the best intentions of others and extending an open mind to them.
- Regularly attending to tiny things for members of your team.
- teaching the skill of rising above a significant setback or disappointment.
- See a synopsis of Dare to Lead that offers additional techniques for enhancing your capacity for vulnerability.

8. Make your expectations clear.

People are more likely to develop trust in the workplace when expectations are clear to them. It's simple to step beyond boundaries when they're unclear. According to a Gallup poll, barely half of workers know what their manager expects of them on the job. By outlining expectations and acceptable behavior, clarity reduces friction and unhappiness at work. It also lets people know what behavior is not acceptable at work. A leader establishes limits that clearly define the parameters under which the team functions.

Try these to prevent any relationship breakdowns at work:
- establishing clear goals for every team member.
- establishing expectations with new hires throughout the orientation phase.
- distributing recommendations using written and spoken

means.

- establishing a regular schedule for finishing the assignment. Every project, for example, cannot be a "rush project."
- Making reasonable schedules.
- ensuring that expectations are mutually understood.
- resolving any ambiguity, queries, or issues with the stated expectations.
- See this chapter for other methods in which leaders might set expectations.

9. Share nothing that you are not authorized to share.

Recovering from a breach of trust, such as disclosing private, delicate, or intimate details and experiences, can be challenging. This could be demonstrated in the workplace by sharing with someone else what you discussed in private with a different team member. People will come to the conclusion that they can't come to you with reliable information if incidents like this continue since you'll overlook it. Worse yet, confidential data can sometimes serve as fuel for detrimental workplace practices like rumors. Team members may experience feelings of rejection, embarrassment, hurt, and devaluation as a result from their coworkers. It is unacceptable to allow this kind of behavior in the workplace.

The result of words and deeds being in harmony is trust. Keep conversations private if you declare them to be so. Sensitive information should be held in a vault, as Brené Brown refers to it when she describes it. Reassure someone who confides in you that you will protect their information or experience. When managing personal information, psychological safety, stability, and predictability are essential for a leader trying to establish trust. When workers observe that you honor your commitments, they feel safe.

10. Make a decision and act with conviction and confidence.

The guiding vision that guides the company's initiatives must be believed in by leaders. Uncertainty and instability result from a CEO who is always doubting their own abilities. Since trust necessitates predictability, none of these circumstances provide a basis for fostering trust. Team members start to feel like they're trapped in the woods at night, waiting for an ambush, when a leader exhibits indecision. Feeling immobile is evident. It causes tension, worry, and fear—all potent ingredients of a poisonous work environment.

Your group must feel confident in your ability to reach the goal and in your ability to implement a strategy. Nobody else will share your belief in your vision if you don't. Employee retention, productivity, and engagement are all impacted by this. Simply put, motivation and inspiration are the two essential elements that will energize others to realize your vision.

Developing trust is a difficult task. In fact, there will be moments when it seems unsettling or scary. For example, this could appear as empathy rather than sympathy when a team member experiences a loss of a loved one. It might also entail having an open discussion on diversity and inclusion in cases where the business hasn't placed a lot of emphasis on it in the past. Leaders who are prepared to be there for their team no matter what gain the trust of their colleagues. They don't only show up in prosperous times. When things get hard, real leaders are the ones that jump in to help. Leading authority on emotional intelligence Daniel Goleman says, "This is a leader who dives into the actual day-to-day functions of the business, as opposed to being the invisible entity who spends his or her time at black-tie CEO events in DC." And that's the kind of leader who inspires confidence.

ACCOUNTABILITY IN CRISIS MANAGEMENT

The significance of responsibility in leadership is more evident at times of crisis. Effective decision-making, transparency, and a high degree of accountability are required of leaders in crisis management. In this thorough investigation, we examine the complex relationship that exists between crisis management and accountability, as well as the vital role that responsible leadership can play in averting disasters.

The Significance of Accountability in Emergencies
1. Open Communication and Informed Decision-Making:

Open communication is the first step towards crisis management accountability. Stakeholders must be kept informed by leaders on the circumstances, the dangers, and the actions being taken. In addition to building trust, this openness offers a framework for group decision-making. Accountable leaders ensure that many viewpoints contribute to well-informed decisions by involving pertinent parties in the decision-making process.

2. Assuming Decision-Making Ownership:

In times of crisis, decisions must be taken quickly and forcefully. Responsible leaders accept responsibility for their choices and own up to their mistakes. This ownership establishes credibility and shows a dedication to growth and learning. In the face of turmoil, leaders inspire confidence and keep things under control by taking accountability for results.

Impediments to Responsibility in Crisis Handling
1. Ambiguity and Uncertainty:

Uncertainty and ambiguity are common characteristics of crisis circumstances. It could be difficult for leaders to make decisions in these kinds of situations and to be held responsible for the results. On the other hand, transparent leadership calls for the recognition of uncertainty in the process of making well-informed choices. Leaders need to explain how the problem is changing and why their decisions were made.

2. Keeping Prudence and Urgency in Check:

The difficulty faced by accountable leaders is striking a balance between the necessity for cautious decision-making and the urgency of crisis response. While leaders rush to address pressing problems, they could miss long-term repercussions. Achieving equilibrium necessitates a sharp understanding of the decisions' immediate and wider effects, guaranteeing responsibility for the results of crisis management.

Accountability Techniques for Crisis Management

1. Getting Ready and Scheduling:

Before a problem arises, accountability must begin. Leaders that make a significant investment in comprehensive crisis planning and preparation are better equipped to react. This entails creating precise procedures, preparing scenarios, and holding frequent exercises to make sure teams are prepared for a range of crisis situations. Reactive decision-making is minimized when readiness is approached pro-actively, which increases accountability.

2. Determining Explicit Duties and Positions:

It is critical to clearly define roles and duties during times of crisis. Team members that are led with accountability are aware of their responsibilities, authority over decisions, and duties. This clarity creates a foundation for accountability, improves coordination, and avoids uncertainty. The value of every team member's contribution to the broader crisis management plan must be made clear by leaders.

3. Accepting Responsibility:

After a crisis, responsible leaders do a detailed examination of what went well and what didn't. The foundation of accountability is the ability to learn from failures. This procedure entails an honest assessment of choices, deeds, and results, producing insights that might guide future crisis management plans. Leaders that actively look for ways to learn from failures show that they are dedicated to never stopping improving.

Crisis Management: Fostering Trust Through Accountability

1. Receptivity to Input:

Team members, stakeholders, and outside sources are all

places where accountable leaders aggressively solicit and appreciate feedback. A culture of constant improvement is fostered by this openness to criticism. Feedback is even more important in times of crisis since it offers instantaneous information that can guide flexible tactics. Prioritizing input shows that a leader is dedicated to accountability and flexible enough to change direction in light of fresh facts.

2. Reliable and Truthful Communication:

In times of crisis, trust is a delicate resource. Honest and regular communication is a top priority for accountable leaders in order to uphold confidence with internal and external stakeholders. This entails giving frequent updates, admitting difficulties, and being open and honest about the decision-making procedure. In the long term, honesty fosters trust, even in the face of bad news.

Accountability's Future in Crisis Management
1. Technology Integration:

As technology advances, responsible leaders are using cutting-edge crisis management solutions. Making decisions more quickly and accurately is made possible by communication platforms, data analytics, and artificial intelligence. To make sure that technical solutions adhere to moral norms and accountability guidelines, leaders must, nevertheless, continue to exercise caution.

2. International Cooperation:

In today's globalized society, problems frequently cut across national borders. Responsible leaders understand the value of international cooperation in handling crises. This entails cross-border sharing of data, assets, and knowledge. It is probable that international collaboration would be given more importance in the future of crisis management responsibility in order to tackle intricate and varied problems.

Under summary, accountability is a critical component of crisis management that can make the difference between a leader's success and failure under trying circumstances. It is not just a catchphrase. The fundamental elements of responsible leadership during times of crisis include open and honest communication, taking responsibility for decisions made, and a dedication to ongoing development. Leaders are able to inspire confidence, overcome obstacles head-on, and effectively and resiliently navigate crises by adopting proactive measures and inspiring trust. Going forward, the amalgamation of technology and worldwide cooperation will significantly mold the terrain of responsible leadership in crisis handling, underscoring the continuous significance of flexibility and moral judgment.

How to Lead Through a Crisis

Professionals across all industries need to know how to lead during a crisis. Leaders that possess these qualities will be able to handle unforeseen problems for the benefit of their organization, its staff, and its clients. Every leader dreams of a stable workplace with defined roles, goals, and procedures as well as established procedures and infrastructure. In the commercial world, this isn't always the case, though. There will always be difficult moments. There will be instances when there will be significant issues that need to be resolved, such as keeping liquidity, managing expenses, handling operational difficulties, and handling staff shortages. During periods of uncertainty, a leader's abilities are put to the test in unexpected ways. Furthermore, amid a crisis only a competent leader can successfully guide an organization. What qualities, then, distinguish effective leaders in these circumstances? These five leadership qualities, which are essential for navigating a precarious corporate environment and knowing how to lead during a crisis, set successful and strong leaders apart from the others in crisis management.

Five Essential Leadership Qualities for Effective Crisis Management:
1. Skillful dialogue
2. Ingenuity
3. Making decisions
4. Dependability
5. Compassion

1. Clear and concise communication

For any organization to function well, effective communication is always essential. That is, however, vitally important while handling a crisis. This is a result of everyone being tense amid a crisis. People always want to know the truth about what is going on, what the authorities are doing to control the situation, and when they should expect things to return to normal. Misinformation is certain to occur in the absence of prompt and transparent communication. Unfortunately, things can go horribly wrong with this. Knowing what, when, and how to communicate is essential for any leader hoping to navigate a crisis, especially when breaking bad news is involved. Here are some pointers for approaching it:

Communicate important information concisely and promptly. When anxiety and worry are running high, it can be difficult to process too much information at once. Just include what is necessary, and do it as soon as you can.

- Be sincere: Effective leaders acknowledge their ignorance. Be forthright about your ignorance and share what you do know.
- Employ a variety of media and communicate often. It's critical that everyone receives the information and comprehends your message when handling a crisis. Make sure you communicate with your team over a variety of channels, including group chats, emails, and in-person meetings. If necessary, repeat the material in many formats and on a regular basis.
- Get ready for questions: Make sure you address any concerns and/or inquiries ahead of time. Still, make sure to pay attention to the queries and worries raised by your staff. When you don't have an answer, be upfront and prepared with what you do know.
- Be human and pay attention: Everyone experiences an emotional rollercoaster during a crisis. Accept your feelings and show empathy for those on your team. Try to establish a human connection with them by listening to what they have to say. In addition to increasing productivity, this kind of communication will inspire your group.

2. Ingenuity

A resourceful person can swiftly adjust to various circumstances and use their imagination to come up with answers. A catastrophe can strike with little to no notice. Do not panic or begin to ponder what to do at this point. An effective crisis leader can seize the moment, make the most of the resources at hand, and lead through a crisis. This includes:

- Seeing beyond the status quo and emphasizing innovative approaches to improve the situation
- Acquiring knowledge and comprehending challenging procedures in an attempt to identify solutions
- Having an open mind to fresh ideas
- maximizing the resources already in place and increasing productivity
- Setting aside organizational resources in anticipation of future emergencies is a sign of readiness.

3. Making choices

Making decisions in crisis management can be difficult but necessary. The decision-making process is impeded by the uncertainty and maybe unprecedented circumstances of the moment, insufficient knowledge, and time constraints. But a competent crisis manager can swiftly assimilate the facts at hand, identify the most important information, and act rapidly to reach a decision. How can you build strong decision-making at the core of your crisis management approach?

- Determine the decision's fundamental goals and the issue it will attempt to resolve.
- Be adaptable and quick to react, especially in situations when things are changing quickly.
- Control your emotions to stay out of trouble or obstacles.
- Have faith in your instincts.
- Proceed now and adjust your approach later if needed.

4. Trustworthiness

The difficulties you have when figuring out how to lead during a crisis might not be within your control. All eyes, however, are on you to provide guidance and guarantee business continuity during this period. It may be necessary for you to take direct responsibility for the issue and consistently deliver in every way. This could entail focusing the team's attention in the same direction, establishing KPIs and other performance measurements, and encouraging team accountability. Every day or every week, ask your department leaders to list their top priorities and report back to you. This will guarantee that you are aware of and in alignment with the priorities. Allow the leaders to monitor performance using the predetermined measures and to keep you informed. Additionally, throughout this time, keep in mind to be accessible and honest about your personal requirements for wellbeing. To guarantee that you maintain your fighting form, pay attention to both your body and mind.

5. Compassion

Empathy is a valuable trait to have when leading through a crisis. During a crisis, you and others are likely to experience intense emotions. But true concern for other people's feelings is crucial if you want to operate as a team and come out on the other side of the crisis with success. Try to put yourself in their position and comprehend their viewpoints. Take the time to hear out their worries. Show compassion and intervene to enable and support their success. Prioritize the mental health of your staff members and let them know how to take care of themselves. But first, you need to address your feelings. Don't pretend that everything is fine when it's not; sometimes admitting your faults makes you seem like a fellow human. Make self-care a priority in order to prepare yourself for the demands of crisis management.

6. Contracting out

Businesses are compelled to reconsider their operations and make strategic changes when faced with a crisis. Here is where outsourcing's advantages really show off: in addition to meeting businesses' immediate needs, it provides them with stability over time, enabling them to grow and adapt as the world around them changes on a regular basis. In this day and age, outsourcing has shown to be a successful business approach for many. Taking on several difficulties at once has been shown to be a fantastic strategy for keeping your business successful and afloat! One excellent technique to do tasks without taking on the workload yourself is by outsourcing.

An effective crisis manager might, for example, choose to contract with a PEO services provider. What exactly are PEO services, then, and how might they help a company in times of need? Payroll, benefits, and other personnel administration activities are all part of the PEO services offered by a professional employer organization. A PEO can intervene in times of crisis to support business continuity by, among other things, processing payroll on time, managing the onboarding of new hires or layoffs, informing on benefits and leave policies, and keeping track of any changes to regulations.

The true test of a leader's qualities and skills comes during a crisis. Nevertheless, competent crisis managers step up to the plate and take charge even in the face of anxiety and uncertainty. The five leadership qualities listed above can assist individuals who are unsure about how to lead during a crisis in adapting and guiding their organizations toward better results. Knowing how to lead during a crisis is made easier by ingenuity, dependability, clear and effective communication, and sound decision-making. Furthermore, demonstrating empathy makes sure that everyone keeps in mind that everyone works in a workplace where people collaborate for the benefit of the team and the business.

Decision-Making under Pressure

Crisis or high-pressure scenarios are common places for leadership to be put to the test. A strong leader's capacity to make judgments effectively under duress is a distinguishing feature. Leaders who can maintain composure and make thoughtful judgments in the face of unforeseen difficulties, pressing deadlines, or an unexpected catastrophe inspire confidence and lead their teams through hardship. When making decisions, pressure can come from a number of places. Time restraints, scarce resources, huge stakes, or outside scrutiny could be the cause. Pressure's effects on the body and mind can impair judgment and cause stress. It is essential for leaders to understand these dynamics in order to create plans to lessen their impact.

Decision-Making and Cognitive Biases:

People are prone to cognitive biases under duress, which can distort how they make decisions. Decision quality can be harmed by common biases including confirmation bias, which is the tendency to favor information that supports preexisting beliefs, and the anchoring effect, which is the tendency for people to depend too much on the first piece of information they come across. Leaders need to be conscious of these prejudices and take proactive measures to lessen their impact.

Emotional Intelligence's Function:
Making decisions under duress is a critical function of emotional intelligence. Emotionally intelligent leaders are able to control their own feelings as well as recognize and comprehend others' feelings with precision. They are able to make decisions that take into account both the emotional and logical components of a situation because of this knowledge. Keeping a clear and concentrated mind is facilitated by acknowledging and controlling emotions.

Research Cases:
Analyzing real-world instances of people making decisions under duress sheds light on the tactics used by effective leaders. The Apollo 13 mission serves as a prime example of the value of cooperation, communication, and adaptation in high-stakes scenarios. During the flight, NASA had to make crucial decisions to safely return the crew to Earth following an oxygen tank explosion.

Developing a Mindset for Resilient Leadership:
One essential quality for leaders handling pressure is resilience. Having a positive mindset, growing mentally tough, and viewing setbacks as chances for personal development are all components of building resilience. Resilient leaders overcome obstacles, motivate their groups, and get back up after failures.

Decision-Making Under Pressure Training:
Programs for developing leaders may include scenarios and simulations that mimic high-pressure situations. Through the ability to experience making decisions under pressure, these training activities help leaders hone their skills and boost their confidence when faced with real-world issues. Self-awareness, planning, and a dedication to lifelong learning are key to developing the talent of making decisions under duress. Outstanding leaders understand the

need of being focused, using emotional intelligence, and taking lessons from past mistakes and accomplishments. Effective decision-making under pressure not only helps organizations overcome obstacles, but it also helps leaders leave a legacy of motivating and guiding their teams to success. Leaders can make decisions with purpose and poise by adopting a resilient mentality, minimizing cognitive biases, and comprehending the dynamics of pressure.

How to Make the Right Decisions Under Pressure

A single choice can lead you to a completely different existence. Your decision could have a cascading effect on numerous aspects of life. It is therefore inherently human to strive to avoid making poor choices. Nevertheless, you frequently don't have time to consider your options while you're under pressure. As a result, we're going to provide you some advice on how to make wise choices under duress.

How to Make the Best Choices When Under Duress

Remain composed.

Stress hormones are released by the body when you're under duress. Positive or negative physiological and mental reactions might also result from it. Your heart will race, and you may experience fear, anger, sadness, or anxiety. Furthermore, emotions have such strong effects that they can affect your actions, behaviors, and ideas, according to specialists. Therefore, you must maintain your composure when under pressure to ensure that you make the best choices. Try these breathing techniques when you're experiencing it. One of the best methods to reduce the amount of stress in your body is to breathe deeply, suggests Michigan Medicine. You can also shift your attention for the time being and unwind before returning to the problem.

Examine the circumstances carefully.

Examine your situation carefully despite the hurry. Power comes from knowledge. Knowing more will help you make better decisions. You want to be aware of all the factors that will impact the overall image. With those, you may now think more clearly, assess your options more effectively, and decide wisely. The added obstacle of making the appropriate judgment at the right time arises when you are under pressure. You run the risk of being too late if you take too long. Making a snap decision could lead to rashness. And occasionally, even though it seems like you don't have time to reflect further, you do. Thus, in these situations, it's critical that you step back, think things through, and then make a decision.

Make a list of every choice you have.

Writing down your possibilities can be helpful if you feel that your ideas are disorganized and you are unable to decide. Your options become clearer and more logical when you put them in writing. In this manner, even under pressure, you'll be able to assess your options more effectively. You can also add the justifications for your decisions next to your selections. Why should you choose it? Why wouldn't you? By doing this, you also avoid making biased decisions.

Get a second opinion.

It's often necessary to view a situation through fresh eyes in order to make the best decisions. Speak with someone you feel comfortable talking to. Maybe it won't occur to you until someone makes it clear to you what you have overlooked. You can relax more when you talk to someone. You reduce the likelihood that your decisions will be influenced by your emotions when you feel more collected.

Concentrate on your objective

This choice you're making will help you get closer to your objectives. The ideal choices won't always be the greatest ones given the circumstances. However, they can also assist you in achieving your goal. You should thus concentrate on your aim rather than the choice. You make a lot of decisions in your daily life. And it can range from minor decisions like what to have for breakfast to major ones that might alter one's entire life. Furthermore, since uncertainty never goes away, you never know when you'll have to make a snap decision. You can make the appropriate decisions if you use the preceding advice.

Maintaining Team Morale during Crisis

Your employees are now acclimating to the brief COVID-19

shutdowns and/or working conditions. There's a risk of sharp drops in output, customer satisfaction and experience, morale, and team effectiveness when people operate remotely or isolate themselves socially in factories and other environments. There is a larger chance of deterioration the longer the span. These are some proactive actions that can be taken to improve morale and productivity.

Daily schedule for correspondence amid the emergency:
1. Make yourself known and speak up

Managers and leaders need to be frequently seen and heard. Take advantage of Zoom and other technologies to ensure that your people see you daily, or more frequently if necessary. Stillness is not bliss; even brief announcements count, especially in times of need. Make team and one-on-one meetings, as well as check-ins, a priority to make sure targets are reached.

2. Exercise transparency
Customers, investors, and employees—the three primary constituencies—are searching for answers, many of which you are unable to provide. It is imperative that leaders maintain a constant, composed demeanor and take deliberate steps with regard to longer-term objectives during this time of uncertainty. Even in situations when information is changing, transparency is essential to preserving confidence. Consider yourself a reporter and give your constituents the who-what-when-where-why information so they won't have to spread tales to fill in the blanks.

Use expressions like these:
"These are the steps we've taken."
"This is how it will impact you and your team."
"This is the rationale for our approach."
"This is the time it will become operative."

3. Have self-assurance
It's normal to get overly preoccupied with managing the volatility. Tell your team members, investors, and clients that they should still have faith in you if they did so one month ago. An workplace that is more productive is created when managers, at all

levels, maintain their focus on what can be done rather than what cannot.

4. Be honest: WFH and temporary settings aren't smooth or attractive. Share it too if you and your partner or children—who are all employed there—are fighting for internet space at home. Workers want to know that you share their trench.

5. Have expectations but be adaptable.

Establish clear expectations for daily production, but be understanding and accommodating to the company's policies. Both psychologically and logistically, crisis WFH conditions are difficult. When any number of family members are present in the house while you're at work, tensions can easily build up (stressors include spouses, younger kids, college-age students returning from semester-long residences, and elder care issues).

6. Morale is important; give them some authority

In uncertain times, morale is not a "nice to have," but rather a need. Anxiety is most commonly experienced when one lacks control. (As an illustration, look no farther than empty store shelves). Let workers experience little wins in the things they can manage, including being able to provide food, supplies, or other help to employees who are badly affected. Give staff members a platform to discuss WFH errors and hacks. Everyone needs to have a sense of humor and patience.

7. Return the favor

Be exemplary corporate citizens both inside the company and outside of it. Businesses that have the ability to help should do it because, a) it is morally correct and, b) the goodwill it creates will outweigh any advertising a company could purchase. Spread the word about this announcement both inside and beyond the company to boost pride in the accomplishments.

8. Inculcate a message of thriving

Because they make do with what they have and frequently take on much larger opponents—including crises—scrappy teams are productive. They are good communicators and always looking for ways to cover each other's blind spots and score points. Encourage the development of a scrappy, problem-solving mindset: It is simple for certain personnel to think in terms of "yes, but...we can't do this or that now" when business is not going as usual. For real, this is a difficult circumstance for all of us. Instead of offering you justifications, challenge your staff to present "yes, and... this is what we can do instead" answers. I picked up this little technique from an expert in improv that can help you think more strategically and look for fresh opportunities that the crisis has brought about. Put them to the test by challenging them to overcome any obstacles. Your personnel following COVID-19

Although this crisis is just momentary, its ramifications will remain longer. It might permanently alter the way that some industries (tourist, tourism, events, etc.) run. As such, new procedures and even new technologies will have to be developed. Your initial 2020 strategy intentions have been marginalized, which means that your personnel needs will change. Following the catastrophe, new opportunities and initiatives will emerge. Having the appropriate personnel in place to carry out those new plans at that point will quicken the return to routine. For some businesses, doing less with more can become the standard.

Think about making an investment in:
• predictive people analytics to learn more about the skill sets that are now present in your company and will be required to fill new or updated roles;
• platforms for learning to retrain or upskill employees;
• mentoring and education for newly appointed and elevated managers; and
• technologies for engagement and communication that may be used in real time to assess and diagnose an organization's health.

Recall that discourse is the essence of communication both now and in the future. Remind them that you're still in this together, listen intently to what they have to say, and take initiative.

CONTINUOUS IMPROVEMENT IN ACCOUNTABLE LEADERSHIP

A basic idea that has gained a lot of popularity in a variety of organizational contexts is continuous improvement. Embracing a culture of continuous improvement becomes crucial for promoting long-term success and growth in the context of leadership responsibility. This strategy entails a continuous dedication to improving organizational structures, procedures, and leadership abilities, fostering a culture that actively searches out and recognizes areas for development.

The Basis for Ongoing Enhancement

Accountability in leadership is inextricably related to a readiness to change and adjust to new situations. In this case, continuous improvement means finding opportunities for improvement even when there aren't any obvious problems. It also means not only addressing what's broken. In order to adopt this proactive strategy, leaders must develop a mindset that sees obstacles as teaching moments and failures as opportunities for growth.

Adopting a Culture of Learning

Organizational learning cultures are valuable, and leaders who place a high priority on them know this. This entails fostering an atmosphere in which errors are viewed as chances to improve and criticism is accepted rather than feared. More accountability among team members is a result of a learning culture's promotion of creativity, adaptability, and a feeling of shared accountability.

Putting Feedback Mechanisms in Place

The regular request for and inclusion of feedback is one of the pillars of leadership accountability's continual improvement. Leaders who get constructive feedback gain important understanding of their areas of strength and growth. Setting a good example for their teams, leaders who actively seek out and act upon feedback show a dedication to both professional and personal growth. Formal feedback systems can be established to create an organized framework for gathering opinions from team members at different levels. Examples of these mechanisms include open-door policy, 360-degree assessments, and regular performance reviews. It's important to gather feedback but also to apply it to goal-setting and improving leadership techniques.

Establishing Objectives and Tracking Results

Clear objectives and a methodical approach to tracking results are necessary for continuous improvement. Accountable leaders establish targets that are both attainable and quantifiable, ensuring that they are in line with the organization's overarching goals and vision. These objectives ought to be SMART—specific, measurable, achievable, relevant, and time-bound. By keeping a regular eye on these objectives' progress, leaders can spot problem areas and make the required corrections. This iterative procedure guarantees that accountability is a continuous commitment to attaining excellence rather than a one-time endeavor.

Flexible Management in a Changing Setting

The modern business environment is evolving quickly, and adaptive leadership is essential to upholding responsibility. Leaders need to be flexible and quick to seize new chances and challenges. Reevaluating strategies and tactics on a regular basis to make sure they continue to support the organization's mission and the changing needs of stakeholders is known as continuous improvement. Leaders that are adaptable recognize that what worked today might not work tomorrow. They keep up with changes in customer behavior, industry trends, and technology developments. Because of this insight, they are able to proactively modify their organizational procedures and leadership style, promoting an accountable culture that is adaptable to changing circumstances.

Making an Investment in Career Advancement

Maintaining leadership responsibility requires a dedication to continuous professional development. Leaders that place a high priority on their personal development through mentorship programs, training courses, and other activities are better able to motivate and steer their staff. Professional development is more than just learning new abilities; it also entails keeping up with industry trends, best practices, and leadership theories. Investing in one's personal development shows that a leader is committed to giving their people the best and most current advice available, which promotes a continuous improvement culture.

Using Technology to Increase Efficiency

Systems and techniques made possible by technological breakthroughs can greatly improve leadership accountability. Leaders may use technology to manage projects more efficiently, analyze data, and communicate more effectively. Digital solution integration can track progress, help find areas for improvement, and make reporting more visible. Leaders that integrate technology into their ongoing strategy for improvement show that they are dedicated to productivity and efficacy. Digital collaboration platforms, data analytics, and automated procedures all support an accountable culture by enabling quicker problem-solving and increased adaptability.

The Significance of Appreciation and Festivity

Acknowledging and applauding accomplishments, no matter how minor, is an essential part of leadership accountability progress. Praise for individual and team accomplishments supports a positive culture and inspires ongoing dedication to excellence. Within the organization, leaders who actively celebrate milestones foster a sense of pride and success. In addition to raising spirits, this encouraging feedback promotes a way of thinking that sees achievement as a process rather than a destination. People are more likely to hold themselves and their peers accountable for continuous improvement in this setting.

Overcoming Obstacles in Constant Enhancement

Even though there are many advantages to constant leadership accountability improvement, there may be certain drawbacks that must be recognized and resolved. Progress can be hampered by a lack of money or time, fear of failure, and resistance to change. Proficient leaders foresee these obstacles and execute tactics to surmount them, exhibiting tenacity and dedication to the ongoing enhancement procedure.

To sum up, achieving continuous improvement in leadership

accountability requires a dynamic, constant commitment to excellence rather than a static goal. Leaders that adopt this approach help their organizations develop a culture of learning, adaptability, and responsibility. Through putting emphasis on feedback, establishing and tracking objectives, funding professional growth, utilizing technology, and acknowledging accomplishments, leaders can establish a culture where ongoing enhancement becomes deeply embedded in the organization's culture. This strategy not only helps each person become a better leader, but it also makes the entire organization more successful and resilient to changing circumstances.

The Role of Feedback in Leadership

Good leadership is a dynamic process of cooperation, communication, and ongoing development rather than just giving orders. Feedback is a vital component that drives this process. Leaders may measure their efficacy, pinpoint areas for development, and cultivate a growth-oriented culture among their teams with the help of feedback. We will examine the importance of feedback in leadership, as well as its several forms and methods for giving and receiving helpful criticism.

Why Feedback Is Essential for Leadership

If you've ever participated in sports, you are undoubtedly well aware of the significance of following through. Coaches often stress that in order for golfers to improve their drives and putts, they must follow through properly. Basketball players who want to improve their form and maximize their percentages must shoot free throws with the proper form, footing, and positioning. Coaches of hockey teams frequently advise their players to follow through on shots in order to maximize accuracy and power. In the same way that persistence is essential for athletes, it is also essential for good leadership. However, for leaders, following through is about consistently checking in with people—including themselves—after a task has been finished, rather than about making a shot or finishing a pass. It all comes down to feedback, mostly.

Effective feedback-giving and -taking, in my opinion, is as crucial for leaders as follow-through is for athletes. Leaders that lack it alienate their people and frequently leave things hanging. Goals can become stuck, and dialogue may come to an abrupt end. However, when feedback is given and received on a regular basis, productivity rises, engagement soars, and businesses become more closely aligned with what makes them distinctive. The most accomplished athletes in the world are aware of how crucial follow-through is to their success because without it, they struggle to make shots or provide their best effort. The same strategy needs to be used by leaders with regard to feedback. In other words, until and unless feedback has been provided and received, no task, no goal, and no successes can be realized.

You understand as a leader that good communication is essential to effective leadership. But you have to realize that communication is a continuous process. It's all about an ongoing dialogue that takes place inside your company; it's not about sporadic talks either. Furthermore, the conversation needs to be led by you. This entails providing feedback on a frequent basis and remaining receptive to criticism regarding your work. That may sound intimidating, but developing a feedback culture is essential if you want to advance both your leadership and your company. Here are a few more points to help you understand why feedback is crucial for modern effective leadership:

1: Employee Engagement Is Enhanced by Feedback

Today's leaders are very concerned with employee engagement. Regretfully, a lot of CEOs are clueless about how to start raising staff engagement. As a result, they wind up investing time and money in projects that have little real impact. And so they find themselves back at Square One, where they began. Here's a secret: fostering a culture of feedback and communication can help you achieve your goals and raise engagement levels swiftly and sustainably.

In actuality, the majority of workers want input from their superiors. In contrast to what is often believed, they actually crave input and get upset when they don't get it. Staff engagement levels increase when managers communicate consistently and offer insightful feedback on a regular basis. Regular feedback-giving also encourages employees to communicate more openly with managers and one another. This is how positive changes in organizational cultures can occur.

2: Receiving feedback increases workers' motivation

Some leaders always battle to keep their team members motivated, and I have a suspicion that these leaders aren't making the most of feedback. When forced to work without feedback for extended periods of time, employees may start to feel irrelevant and alienated. Their drive consequently tends to evaporate, which lowers output and lowers the standard of work produced overall. Supervisors who often provide and receive feedback observe that their staff members are more driven. They are aware of the significance of their work and the concern their superiors have for it. Not only are motivated workers more efficient, but they also exhibit higher levels of happiness and engagement.

3: Career Development Is Made Possible via Feedback

Leading is about guiding the ship. However, it's equally crucial that you make sure that there are others who can take on leadership roles. Developing the careers of those you manage is one of the most important things you do for your company, and it simply cannot be done without feedback. Each member of your team has their own personal ambitions, objectives, and professional goals. A lot of them plan to advance in their jobs in ways that will position them for management and the possibility of taking on more responsibility. It is this that sustains an organization's success over years, even decades. But without the ability to provide and accept feedback, leaders such as yourself cannot accomplish any of this kind of progress.

4: Acknowledgment Boosts Leader Performance

Giving others comments will be your main responsibility in this regard. If leaders want to genuinely foster a culture of communication, they must also be receptive to criticism. You should make it a point to ask for input from your staff since you never know when they might feel comfortable providing it. Your team members will be more willing to open up and share their thoughts on your leadership if you encourage feedback. It provides them with the chance to communicate what aspects of your leadership style work and what doesn't. Naturally, it is your responsibility to act upon the feedback you get in a way that communicates to your audience that you are paying attention. By doing this well, you demonstrate to your team members that you care about them and that your leadership is about ensuring the smooth and efficient operation of the company, not about yourself.

Types of Leadership Feedback:

1. Favorable Comments:

Desired behaviors and results are acknowledged and reinforced when they receive positive feedback. It acts as a catalyst, elevating spirits and inspiring team members to keep performing to the best of their abilities. In order to foster a pleasant work environment, leaders ought to acknowledge and commemorate accomplishments of all sizes.

2. Suggested Improvements:

The goal of constructive criticism is to raise performance. It provides insights on how people might increase their effectiveness by focusing on particular activities or behaviors that require modification. Good leaders emphasize progress over criticism and offer helpful criticism in a constructive way.

3. Comment from 360 degrees:

Gathering input for this type entails speaking with peers, bosses, and subordinates, among other people. A leader's performance is seen in its entirety through 360-degree feedback, which presents a balanced picture of their strengths and opportunities for improvement. It encourages self-awareness and a comprehensive strategy for developing leadership skills.

Techniques for Giving Helpful Feedback

1. Reliability:

Feedback given on time has more impact. When giving feedback, leaders should try to match it as closely as possible to the performance or behavior that was seen, so that team members can relate the comments to particular actions.

2. Details:

More actionable feedback is specific. Leaders should give specifics about what was done well or where improvement is required, as opposed to making generalizations. People are more able to comprehend the context and make targeted modifications when given specific instances.

3. Equipped Method:

It is important to acknowledge both your talents and your room for progress in a balanced approach. It is the goal of leaders to foster a pleasant environment by acknowledging accomplishments and finding constructive solutions to problems.

4. Consistent Visits:

Giving and receiving feedback is a continuous process. Leaders have the opportunity to assess progress, provide direction, and make necessary strategy adjustments via routine check-ins. Open communication and trust-building are fostered by consistent communication.

Techniques for Getting Feedback Well:

1. Adaptability:

Leaders need to have an open mind when it comes to feedback. Instead of taking offense, they ought to see criticism as a chance for improvement. A culture where feedback is viewed as a tool for progress rather than as criticism is fostered by a responsive mindset.

2. Listening Actively:

Accurately interpreting feedback requires active listening. Leaders ought to pay close attention, seek clarification where necessary, and make an effort to completely understand the viewpoints of people offering criticism. This encourages open conversation and shows respect for other people's viewpoints.

3. Ongoing Education:

It is imperative to adopt a mindset of perpetual learning. Positive or constructive criticism should be viewed by leaders as an opportunity to improve their leadership abilities. This proactive methodology facilitates continuous professional growth.

4. Further Measures:

Not only do competent leaders take in input, they also act upon it. Leaders that act on comments and make necessary adjustments show that they are dedicated to development and advancement. It also supports the notion that constructive criticism is an effective means of promoting change.

Feedback is essential to leadership since it fosters growth, improves team communication, and offers insights. Leaders who foster a climate of constructive criticism help create a productive workplace where people feel appreciated and encouraged to advance their careers. The secret is to embrace feedback with an attitude of constant growth and a dedication to establishing solid, cooperative teams, whether you are giving or receiving it. People can increase their effectiveness and help their teams and organizations succeed overall by incorporating feedback into their leadership practices.

CONCLUSION

We have examined the many dimensions of what it means to be a truly accountable leader as we have journeyed through the pages of this book on accountable leadership. The tremendous effects of responsible leadership ripple out from the leader to the very foundation of their companies and, in turn, to society at large. It is critical to consider the most important lessons learned and the future-changing potential that accountability carries as we come to the end of this thorough investigation. As we have explained, **Accountability** is a fundamental component of good leadership, not just a catchphrase. It is the cornerstone around which decisions are made, trust is established, and long-term success is attained. We have explored the fundamental ideas of accountable leadership in these chapters, highlighting the significance of morality, values, and an environment that encourages accountability.

The idea of **transparency** is one of the main ideas this book explores. Transparent leadership goes beyond merely disseminating facts; it also involves creating an atmosphere in which candid communication is expected. Transparent leaders foster an atmosphere of trust and genuineness, which empowers their teams to overcome obstacles with resiliency and resolve. Going forward, it is imperative for leaders to acknowledge that transparency plays a crucial role in establishing and preserving connections, both inside and beyond their establishments. Another important theme that runs across these chapters is the creation of a **culture of accountability.** A culture that promotes accountability enables individuals and teams to flourish in all aspects of their lives, from goal-setting and accomplishment to accepting responsibility and conquering obstacles. It is incumbent upon us as leaders to establish and maintain this culture. Creating an atmosphere where each member has a sense of ownership and is aware of how their activities affect the success of the group as a whole takes time and work.

As a guiding concept in the quest for accountable leadership, **continuous improvement** stands out. Feedback is a useful tool for growth, not something that leaders should interpret as criticism. Leaders may improve their decision-making abilities, hone their talents, and adjust to the constantly changing nature of leadership by proactively soliciting and incorporating feedback. What sets exceptional leaders apart from mediocre ones is their dynamic, iterative path towards constant improvement.

We have seen throughout these chapters how vital **trust** is to effective leadership. Earning trust requires constant responsibility, open communication, and a strong dedication to moral behavior. As leaders, we have to acknowledge that trust is brittle and that it takes a determined effort to restore when it has been damaged. Leaders may establish robust and long-lasting relationships with their teams, stakeholders, and the wider community by giving priority to techniques that foster trust. Accountable leadership is characterized by the capacity to manage and guide through **crises.** Accountable leaders step up to the plate when things get unclear, making morally-driven choices and providing resilient team leadership. The takeaways from crisis management emphasize the value of readiness, flexibility, and a resolute dedication to fundamental values even in the face of difficulty. As we get to the end of our investigation, it is critical to recognize that responsible leadership is an ongoing process rather than a static position. Leadership is going to be shaped by people who can adapt to change, stay flexible, and always want to do better. The landscape of leadership will continue to change due to emerging trends, opportunities, and challenges, and responsible leaders must be prepared to meet these changes head-on with bravery and conviction.

Let's embrace the spirit of this book and see the end not as a point of departure but rather as a fresh start. Equipped with the wisdom and insights presented in these pages, leaders can set out on a path of ongoing development, generating beneficial ripple effects inside their companies and throughout the wider community. It is very evident what needs to be done: show responsible leadership, motivate others around you, and help build a prosperous and sustainable future. By working together as responsible leaders, we can successfully negotiate the challenges of our dynamic environment and create a lasting legacy of effective leadership.

BE ACCOUNTABLE!